John Saunders

Martin Pole

Vol. 1

John Saunders

Martin Pole
Vol. 1

ISBN/EAN: 9783743340794

Manufactured in Europe, USA, Canada, Australia, Japa

Cover: Foto ©ninafisch / pixelio.de

Manufactured and distributed by brebook publishing software (www.brebook.com)

John Saunders

Martin Pole

MARTIN POLE.

BY

JOHN SAUNDERS,

AUTHOR OF "ABEL DRAKE'S WIFE," ETC.

IN TWO VOLUMES.

VOL. I.

LONDON:

TINSLEY BROTHERS, 18, CATHERINE ST., STRAND.
1863.

PREFACE.

THE parts of MARTIN POLE entitled "Old Matthew's Puzzle," the "Haunted Crust," and "Julian," are by my daughter; the first having been written at the age of sixteen.

Having in the last edition of ABEL DRAKE'S WIFE, recently published, expressed my sense of the favour with which that book had been received, and my hope to show by its successor (which I expected to issue by the autumn), that I did not misunderstand my welcome, it may be as well now to add, that the work thus referred to was not MARTIN POLE, which belongs essentially to an earlier period.

JOHN SAUNDERS.

JUNE, 1863.

CONTENTS OF VOL. I.

———◆———

	PAGE
UNDER THE LINDEN TREES .	1
THE SENTENCE . .	17
THE MORNING OF THE DAY .	31
THE PLAGUE-STONE OF ABERFORD	53

MARTIN POLE.

UNDER THE LINDEN TREES.

That's my name, sir, Matthew Mucklethrift, and two t's in the Matthew, if you would be so kind; I shouldn't mention it, only I once had a sharp escape of losing a bit of money a master of mine left me, all through a rascally lawyer cutting me off with one t. Well, sir, as to these stories we are talking about. I don't boast. God forbid I should, when I may be carried off any minute with one of these rheumatic fits; but somehow, there seems no one in the parish that's been allowed to see so many stories right through as I have. It's like Abel Jenner's three sons and the apple-tree with most of 'em. It was the biggest apple-tree in the country, and Jenner always said he'd give it to his eldest son. And so he did, for a christening present, when it was all covered with good, firm blossom, without a blight. But the little one and the blossom went off together. In a year and a half Jenner had another son to give it to. Well, the child lived to see it covered with little hard, green apples, but before one of them was ripe, he died. A few years on, the third was born, and Jenner gave his tree to him. The leaves were falling off it then, and before they came on again, he was laid along with his two little brothers in the new burial-ground. And so it is, I say, with stories. One man sees the beginning of a story, and dies; another the middle and dies; and another the end; while, as for me, I seem to stand by, as if old death had forgotten me, and see the blossom, the fruit, and dead leaves, and all.

And now, before I begin, I should take it very kindly if you would just state the reason of my being obliged to be beholden to you for writing this, instead of doing it myself. The truth is, sir, schools in my day were not what they are now.

All the scholarship that ever I had was got at a wretched little place standing by itself on the moor, kept by one Johnny Cotterel, a lame young man, not quite right in his head, for he used to sit behind his high desk and scribble poetry from morning till night, and was always in love with one or other of the Squire's daughters.

In winter the school-house, being quite exposed on the moor, was so cold that Johnny Cotterel was forced to flog us all round when first he came of a morning, to get a bit of warmth into his fingers; and, though we didn't take to it particularly, I don't see how our circulations would have gone on without it. In summer it was that hot, and Johnny Cotterel used to get so touchy in his head that he couldn't keep that little whisking cane of his still two minutes together; and as for the bread and butter, sir, that we used to take for dinner, you could almost hear it frizzle on the shelf; and it tasted as strong of geography as ever it could taste.

He was a character was Johnny Cotterel; and if it's true, sir, what you were kind enough to mention, about my observing people pretty deep without them knowing it, the foundation of the talent was laid at Johnny Cotterel's school. For, I should tell you, that while he sat with his hands stuck through his hair, and his eyes rolling in his head as if he'd got a thought wedged in half-way that he couldn't move in nor out, Johnny had a nasty knack of letting fly with his cane right into the middle of us, and laying about him as if he were mad. The fits came on him all of a sudden with a big thought, or when he was hard put to it for a rhyme, so that the boys never knew how to be even with him. But, as for me, bless you, I observed him in that way that I soon got to know the roll of his eye in good time, and to make for the slate-cupboard like a dart.

Ah, poor Johnny Cotterel! But I've run on too much about him already, only I wanted to show you that schools like his weren't exactly the places for promoting knowledge, however good they may have been for the circulation, that's all; and now, if you're ready, sir, I'll take the liberty of beginning.

When I came to Throgmorden Manor-house as head-gardener, my master, Squire Pole, was just sixty-five years old; so you may think I was a little surprised to hear, a week after I had been there, that he rode over every evening on his white mare to court a lady at Chistledean.

At first none of us at the Manor-house, as we saw him go off frilled and perfumed, could make out who the lady was; for Chistledean was but a poking little place then, with only two respectable houses in it—the rectory, and King Combe, an estate belonging to a family named Hilman. As the parson had only his wife and mother living with him, the attraction couldn't have been there; but then how could it have been at King Combe, we used to say, and look grave; for the lady of King Combe had only been a widow six months, and was supposed to have been a most devoted wife; besides which, she had a young son to

bring up; and altogether it was more than any
of us would have liked to say that Mrs. Hilman
was the Squire's attraction.   However, it was not
a secret very long.   The thing was made known
in this way.   When I had been at the Manor-
house two months, it suddenly came out that
Mrs. Hilman was not worth a penny : Hilman's
affairs had just been settled in London, and every
inch of King Combe was to be sold to pay
his debts.   Then the question was, what would
the poor widowed lady do to keep herself and
her little son: she who had never turned her hand
to a bit of work since she was born?   What *did*
she do?   Why, just married Squire Pole; and
stepped out of King Combe into the Manor-house
as comfortably as if her husband had been dead
seven years, instead of seven months to a day.

You may be sure that all this made no little
talk in Throgmorden and Chistledean for long
enough to come; and my Mistress Pole was
spoken of in rather a light manner by those who
had believed her to be so devoted to her first
husband; and some said she must have cared for

the Squire before Mr. Hilman died. But then her maid Rance told us one day something that seemed to make that not very likely. Rance, in unpacking a box that had not been opened since her lady went into mourning, let fall a little framed portrait of Mr. Hilman just at her mistress's feet; and at the sight of it, coming so suddenly upon her, she fainted dead away.

She was a fine woman was my Mistress Pole, with blue eyes and full clear cheeks, and a pile of flaxen curls over each brow; and her figure and her sweeping walk might have belonged to a queen. She was proud too, and had a habit of staring straight at you without seeming to see you when she met you in the grounds or anywhere. I don't know that she ever condescended to speak to me at all, till one day, about five years after she had been married to the Squire, and three months before her second son was born, a little thing happened—at least, I thought it a little thing then—that made her change her manner to me always afterwards.

It was on a hot June evening, the girls had

gone to the fair, the Squire was dining out, and my Mistress Pole was pleased to take a walk by herself in the grounds.

I was at work at a side bed just in sight of the gates, and she took her walk from the linden trees to the gates and back, and so on for a long time, taking no more notice of me than if I'd been a worm. By-and-by I look up and I see a woman putting her hand through the gates and begging of my Mistress Pole. But she walks straight up to the gates as if to speak to the woman, then turns round and walks away, taking no sort of notice of her. Then the beggar, a gipsy woman in a dull scarlet cloak, pushes open the gate that was unfastened, and follows my mistress down the walk, still holding forth her hand and crying to her in a wailing, yet half-threatening voice for charity.

But my Mistress Pole was not a charitable woman in those days; and all she did was to wave her hand in a quick, queenly way, without making a step slower or faster in her sedate, proud walk.

The gipsy took a look round as she followed her, and seeing no one near,—for I suppose the lindens hid me,—made a clutch at her mantle. Then my mistress turned all white with passion, and stamped her foot and cried—

" Begone ! "

And she turned and walked on again; but before I got up to them, the gipsy clutched her mantle again, and this time my mistress shrieked as if she were being murdered.

I soon had hold of the baggage, and pinned her arms to her sides, and marched her off by the same way she had come, without anything worse than the mark of her teeth on my hand; and when she was safe outside the gates, my Mistress Pole called after me, so that she should hear,

" Give her to understand that the next time she is found inside these gates I shall have her horsewhipped."

The gipsy listened to these words with her back towards us in contempt, then she turned and caught hold of the ironwork of the gate with

both hands, and clenched her teeth at my Mistress
Pole, and said, curtseying low,

"Ah, yes, my gentle lady, she understands.
O, she understands, my queen! she understands!"

My mistress then went on with her walk, not so
much as giving me a "thank you;" and when I
had made the gate fast, I went back to my work.

After I had finished, I went in doors, leaving
my mistress still taking her walk from the linden
trees to the gates, and back from the gates to the
linden trees.

By-and-by the servants came home from the
fair, all except one, who was stopping at the field-
gate to have her fortune told. This made me
speak of what had happened, and warn them not
to let any one of the gipsies in, or my Mistress
Pole would surely have them horsewhipped.
When the girl who had stayed behind came in,
she looked so confused with her fine fortune, I
suppose, that I made no doubt she had forgotten
to shut the field-gate after her; and on going to
see, I found it, sure enough, standing wide open.

I shut it, and looked across the field to see if the fortune-teller might be the same gipsy who had insulted my Mistress Pole; but she must have made good use of her legs any way, for she was gone clean out of sight.

It could scarcely have been half an hour after this that the Squire came home, and, as usual with him for some weeks past, inquired particularly after my mistress,—how was she? The lady's maid, who really knew nothing about her, answered the Squire that she was very well this evening, for she had been taking quite a long walk in the grounds. "*Where* was she?" The lady's maid thought very likely in her own room, as she would be tired after her walk.

It seemed, however, that my Mistress Pole was neither in her own room nor in any room of the house, and a fine uproar we were presently in. Every place was searched; and the old Squire came out to me with a lantern, and sent his voice down all the paths calling "Ursula! Ursula!" till he was hoarse.

In the midst of our confusion, suddenly the

girl who had stayed behind to have her fortune told recollected to have seen her mistress from the field-gate sitting down to rest under the linden trees.

We went up to the seat, and it was empty; but down on the grass just before it, all of a heap, and with the fringe of her mantle torn, Mistress Ursula Pole lay in a deadly swoon.

They carried her in and sent for a doctor; and they say that when she came to herself her screams were something frightful. It was even many days before any dared question her concerning the cause of her swooning; and then, when the Squire did at last very gently ask her about it, they tell me my Mistress Pole was seized with fits, and could only be quieted by a promise that they would ask her no more. Of course I told the Squire all I knew about the gipsy, and he ordered that she should be found and punished; but the day on which my mistress had been insulted by her was the last day of the fair, and the whole tribe had gone off, and were on the tramp far enough away by that time.

And so the cause of my Mistress Pole's swooning under the linden trees, and the tearing of her mantle, was hushed up; and, though I thought much and made many guesses concerning it, I never knew the truth till twenty years afterwards. Yes, it was hushed up; but from that time I noticed that whenever my Mistress Pole walked in the grounds she carried a little pouch of money in her hand, and if any asked charity of her, gave it readily; and her word to every one about her was so civil and meek, you could find no reason strong enough to account for such a change.

But not only had her pride been broken down, —for, mind you, she wasn't really a woman of strong intellect: her will, like, was all on the surface,—but from that day her clear pink cheek got paler and paler, her blue eyes hollow, and her flaxen curls mixed with threads of silver. She was given to fits too. The sound of a harsh voice, or even a sudden glare of colour, such as a huntsman's scarlet coat, made her shrink and laugh and sob in a manner fearful to hear; and we all thought she would surely pine and die before her child was born.

Certainly my Mistress Pole had done little to make her people fond of her; but I think I can answer for it that there was no one in the Manor-house, or in all Throgmorden, for that matter, who didn't feel glad when one fine morning,—it was the 28th of August, exactly three months after the last day of the fair,—the bells of Throgmorden and Chistledean rang out the joyful news that a son and heir was born to Squire Pole.

And they named him Martin.

THE SENTENCE.

Now all that I know of Martin Pole till he was twenty years old I can tell you in a very few words.

He was a pale and sickly child, not near so engaging as his little half-brother, James Hilman, but I liked him better; and he used to follow me about, and talk and read to me for hours together. As for my Mistress Pole, she got round a little; but it seemed as if she would never be the same woman I saw that June evening walking backwards and forwards from the linden trees to the gates. It was curious to watch her and Martin. There would be him sitting in his little arm-chair in the garden reading, and his mother, perhaps, on the seat behind him with her 'broidery. Then suddenly she would clench her two hands together, and fix her eyes on the boy, and her lips would turn as white that you could but think she saw something going to fall on him. And, wonderful to say, that child, though he'd have his back towards her, would seem to *feel* that look of hers, and turn slowly round and meet her eye, and shudder from head to foot.

She still had those strange fits, too, when she seemed to be struggling with some one. When little Martin knew her to be taken with one of them it was impossible to keep the child away, and afterwards he was almost as much upset as herself.

One day the child said to me—

"Matthew, your legs shake so, and your hair is so white, I should think you must be very old and wise. Do you think you could answer a very hard question?"

"And what might that be, my little sir?" said I.

He got on the rail of my chair and held me by the collar, while he whispered—

"What is it my mother thinks she hears in those fits that makes her put her fingers in her ears and scream so?"

I could not tell him; and he hoped I might be older and wiser by the time he came back from school, as he very much wanted to have that question answered. So he said.

Well, time went on. The lads were sent to school together; and at sixteen Martin came home ill. Squire Pole died; and after that Mistress Pole and Martin spent all their time together.

Martin never spoke to me about his mother's fits again, though she had them as often as ever; but he used to ponder by himself and watch her, and I don't know which of the two was the most ailing and nervous, Martin or his mother. Then a time came when he was determined to try to rouse himself, and shake off the evil spell there seemed upon him. He went to college and studied hard for four years, and got on famously, I'm told; but came home at twenty, more broken down and ill than ever I had seen him.   His half-brother, James Hilman, was now his agent; and was always so attentive to him that one would never suppose he had the least feeling of envy to be himself so poor while Martin was to inherit a large fortune.

I told you that when Martin was twenty years old I came to hear what it was befell my Mistress Pole under the linden trees that night, and which wrought so wonderful a change in her. Well, I have now come to that.

It was a hot afternoon, much the same kind of afternoon as it had been on the memorable day of Throgmorden fair, before our young master was born.   The Manor-house was gloomy and dark, and nearly all the blinds were down; for Mistress Ursula Pole lay on her bed sick, nigh unto death.

The doctor had been with her many hours, and had left her quiet at last, forbidding her sons to go near her; for, if she slept, all might yet be well.   But scarcely had he ridden out of the gates than the nurse came running to tell me that my Mistress Pole desired to speak with me. Much taken aback by such a message, I went up.

At first I scarcely knew her, she had so wasted away. She was lying back on the pillows, with both her thin hands pressed tightly on her chest, as if every breath was a pain to her. Her cheeks and eyes, bright with fever, I remember looked so strange with her thin white hair and hollow temples. When I stood by the bedside she looked at the nurse and pointed to the door; and then, when she had gone away and left us alone, my Mistress Pole laid her thin hand on my sleeve cuff and drew herself up, and sat looking in my face till her bright wild eyes made mine ache again.

"Matthew," she said, "look at me. They tell me you called me a proud, hard woman once. Do I look that now? Or do I look as if I'd suffered for my hardness and my pride?"

"You look a very wretched woman, Mistress Pole," I said, "and that is all; and if any-thing can be done to put your mind at rest I am glad that you have chosen me, that have been here longer than any one in the house, to do it."

"I know that," she said, quickly. "That is why I sent for you, because you were here so long ago; because you were here *that day*. Do you remember that day, more than twenty years ago, when a woman came a-begging of me at the gates?"

I remembered it well, and told Mistress Pole so; also that she had desired me to horsewhip the woman if she ever came again; also that Mistress Pole had had a bad faint under the linden trees that night; and no sooner had I said the words than she began to tremble and put her hand to her ear, as she always did when that day was spoken of; and she had a hard matter to speak as she clutched the cuff of my sleeve in her hand, and said to me—

"Matthew, she came back to me that night. I had been sitting in the dusk and looking at the moon, which was all red and fiery, over the house. I had sat there till I was almost afraid to move, for I was superstitious, and had lived among superstitious people all my life, and believed in signs and tokens. I had been told that when the moon was as red as it was that night, it is a sign of death, and murder, and all kinds of horrible things. I was cold, but I could not stir. I heard some one, I think it was the girl Phœbe, going past, but I could not call to her; so I sat still, faint and shivering, hoping some of you might come to look for me. But I was left alone; and the air seemed to grow heavier, and the moon redder. Matthew, Matthew, it was hideous! Where it came from I cannot tell; but there it was—her face—her hideous, handsome gipsy face close to mine; it was as if the red moon had changed into it, and approached me. I got up, but my feet seemed turned to lead, and she flung her wiry arms round me and muttered in my ear, '*Lady, did you ever hear a gipsy's curse?*' And her hold of me got tighter and tighter, till I thought I should be suffocated; and then she spoke her curse. O! such a tide of hellish words, I thought it must be a fiend speaking them; and her hot breath seemed to

brand each one on my ear. And those words
made up such a doom for one poor human crea-
ture—a doom more horrible than the world has
ever known; and not for me, O, Matthew! not
for me, but for my babe—my little unborn babe!
'*Not yet,*' she said, '*not yet the curse shall fall;
but when the day of his birth shall have come
round twenty times and one, then let him tremble,
for it is his day of doom. And I shall come and
see the working of my curse; ay, I tell you I will
be there. It may be not till the last day, but I will
be there. It may be not till the last hour, but look
for me then. It may be not till the last second of
the striking of the clock, but even then look for
me; for on that day, though it be at the last
second, I will be there.*'"

When Mistress Pole finished telling me the
gipsy's words, which seemed as fresh in her mind
as if she had heard them twenty hours ago instead
of more than twenty years, she fell back on her
pillow, and lay looking at me, trembling so that
the tarnished gold fringe of the bed-hangings
shook. I thought she seemed surprised, poor

soul, that I was not more horrified by what she had told me; but, whatever I might have felt, I did my best to keep quiet. When she had been still a minute or so, I asked her had she told either of her two sons this?

"I told James," she said. And then I asked her—

"And not Martin? I am glad of that."

But before she could answer me a hand was laid on my shoulder, and when I looked up I saw Martin Pole standing beside me.

He had heard all.

Mistress Pole stared at him wildly, and then cried out—

"O, what have I done! what have I done!" and buried her face in the pillow. Martin went round to his mother's bedside and took her hand; and one look at his face, which was pale as a ghost, but firm, and with something like a smile on it, showed me I might leave him to comfort and talk to his poor foolish mother, so I came out of the room.

I came away, but I couldn't rest two minutes

together for thinking of what my Mistress Pole had had upon her this twenty years. Ah, we little know what one another have to bear. If she had told me this at first, do you think I wouldn't have beat the bushes from here to Canterbury but what I'd have brought that cursing gipsy baggage to gainsay all her gibberish in half the time she had taken to say it?

I could understand how it was she told me now, because, for all the doctor had said, I had seen at a glance, when I went into her bedroom, my Mistress Pole was not long for this world; and it must have been a hard thing for her, after she had lived for twenty years with a knowledge of this, to be called away at last within a year of the day on which Martin was doomed. And though, as she said, she had told James Hilman, it was natural enough she should want an older eye than his to take her place in watching over Martin; and I had been with her twenty years and more, poor body—twenty years and more!

While I was thinking over these things on the bench outside my lodge, I saw Martin's horse led up to the house door, and presently came Martin himself. My Mistress Pole is worse, I thought, and he is going for the doctor. I was right.

When he passed me, as I stood holding the gate open, he coloured a little, and, stooping down, said—

"I know I need not ask you, Matthew, not to mention anything of this. My mother is worse —too ill to be reasoned with; but, now we know her secret, I am sure we can soon rid her of this horrible superstition. What do you say, Matthew?"

I *said* nothing, but I suppose I *looked* as if I thought that Mistress Pole would soon be beyond all our reasoning, for something flashed in his quick, bright eyes, and he turned sharply through the gate and rode away.

Ten days after this, young Martin sat listening to the ding-dong of his mother's funeral bell. His face was pale and thin, with something more than grief. It had been a fearful time for him; and the night of her death was a night which not a soul who was in the Manor-house will ever forget; no, not if they live to twice my age, will one of them forget that night.

All down the long passage where we servants stood listening in the dark came their two voices : my Mistress Pole's weak, broken voice, crying out against death, beseeching Heaven that she might live a little longer, for Martin's sake, to be with him on the day of his doom, as she persisted in calling his twenty-first birthday; and Martin's voice, strong and gentle, breaking in upon her shrill wail, with comforting words, and good, sound, scholarly, and manly reasoning. But that superstition which had grown into her very nature was not to be thrown off at death's door. For one moment, as he tried to show her how impossible it was for a mere woman, let her be gipsy or gentle, to set her will above that Will that orders all things, perhaps for one moment she would seem to take comfort and grow quiet; but in the next, another kind of fright seized on her. She had heard strange stories of gipsy vengeance; the woman might bring her prophecy to pass without any superhuman help; and, supposing this so, careful guard and watching such as *she* might have kept over him on the appointed day, would have been the only means for saving him. A foolish fancy, of course, but real enough to her, poor soul!

I got into the room for a short time, and her moans and cries of agony were almost too much for me to bear, so what must poor Martin have suffered! Instead of his reasoning doing away with her fear, it seemed now, by the deathly whiteness of his face, that her fear was overcoming him, and his head bent lower and lower as she cried out with her last strength—

"Let me live, O, only till that day! Martin, she will come, I know she will come, and you will take no care. You will not believe, but I tell you she will make her curse fall! There was power in her eye—I feel it yet; there was power in her voice!—hark!"

And Mistress Pole fell a listening, and a look of horror came on her face as if some one were speaking in her ear whom she couldn't push off. Then she touched Martin's arm as he knelt by the bed, and beckoned him that he should rise and bend his ear to her. He was so faint and overcome he could scarcely get up. When he did, she did not whisper, but said in a hard, rattling kind of voice, which I had never known the like of before—

"It's all coming dark to me—pitch dark; a noise is in my ears; but you hear me say this, I *command you to take care that day!* She is near us now. I heard her say again—'*Not yet,*' she said—'*not till the last day, may be not till the last hour, the last second of the striking of the clock; but even then, look for me, for on that day, though it be at the last second, I will be there!*' and, Martin, she *will*—I know it."

They were the last words Martin heard her speak, for she was carried off in a faint.

They were her last words, but before she had stopped breathing, a smile came on her face that made it look quite young and fair; so I thought perhaps In that darkness she tells of, she sees a light at last, poor soul!

THE MORNING OF THE DAY.

—•—

It was the 28th of August.

At five o'clock in the morning I was sitting on my lodge bench, looking at the house.

"Twenty times and one" the linden trees had darkened since that June night when a woman came a-begging at the gates. "Twenty times and one" the gipsy fire had left a round black patch in Throgmorden Hollow. "Twenty times and one" the day of Martin Pole's birth had come round.

Now, except in the matter of crows—one meaning bad luck, two good luck, and three a wedding—no one can say I am superstitious; but I must own that, though all the crows came in twos that morning, I felt, as I sat on my bench under the Judas tree, that I would give my silver pot that I won at the rose show and my old clasp-

knife, if this day—this 28th of August—were but
safely over and gone.

However, as yet it was only five by Throgmorden church; and, as I couldn't get at my
breakfast ale till seven, I had two hours to sit
and think of what sort of state we were in at the
Manor-house to meet this day.

We couldn't very well have been in a worse.

Now, first, as to young Martin himself. Bad,
very bad, indeed. He had been getting more and
more ill, so that for the last six weeks he had
hardly stirred from his bedchamber; and never
saw any one but his half-brother, and his own
man Fletcher, a regular walking post, who never
knew how his master was if you asked him.
Certainly this was a queer state of things for such
a day to be met with; and, as I say, it made me
feel very anxious.

"What could it be at the root of Martin's
incessant illness?" I asked myself.

Ever since his mother's death, Martin had
been a mystery to me. He had no disease; Dr.
Oldways was certain of that—at least no bodily

disease; but had he a worse? Had his mother's superstition come upon him in spite of himself? I could not tell, but if it had, it was not the same kind of fear as hers. Martin, you remember, was a scholar,—such a scholar that they say there was no coming to the bottom of his learning, it was so deep. Well, then, if there was any such fear in him, I make it out in this way: not, you understand, that Martin believed the gipsy's curse could have any effect on him of itself, but that, through his mother and before his own will could prevent it, the very mainsprings of his life and energy had been affected; and then the strangeness and mystery of the thing was enough to keep his mind incessantly pondering over it; till he got to be like one entangled in a bad dream,—always trying to wake and throw it off, but always falling back into it again directly.

It would no doubt have been much better for him if he had been obliged to stir about and do something; but, you see, after the death of the old Squire, Mr. James got the management and cares of the estate so entirely into his own hands

that Martin was left with nothing whatever to
do, when he wasn't studying at his books, but
ponder over his mother's story, and count the
hours till the appointed time.

And, now that I have mentioned Mr. James, I
may as well say that, odd as you may think it, I
thought more of him that morning as I sat under
the Judas tree than I did of Martin Pole.

He was that kind of man you could neither
like nor dislike : a mere business machine, coming
in and going out at regular times. He was so
engrossed in doing Martin's work that he seemed
to have no affairs of his own. You couldn't like
his looks, nor you couldn't find fault with them ;
for he was just a middle-sized darkish man, with
a close mouth; and eyes that, wherever they
looked, seemed to see nothing but a row of
figures to add up. His head always projected a
little forward, as if to show the tenantry that it
did all business by itself, and the heart was not
a partner, and could have nothing to do with it.
His step was a patient, plodding sort of step, as
though he wished for no higher walk in life than

always to be his brother's servant, and have the accounts correct. There was nothing but what he would do for Martin; he seemed the one and only soul he cared for in the world; and he often sat up with him, night after night, when he was ill, and tended him like a mother.

Mr. James being this ordinary kind of man, you will wonder how he came to be in my thoughts so much that morning. Well, a very strange thing had happened him. He had dropped his pocket-book. I saw it lying at the side of the walk when I first opened my door in the morning. Now, I had known Mr. James ever since he was a little boy, and had never seen him drop a thing out of his pocket in his whole life before; and when I saw that lying in the path, it seemed a stranger omen of disaster than Mistress Pole's red moon. It was so out of character with the man, that I kept turning the pocket-book over and over in my hands, hardly sure that I was quite awake. Why, I had seen him opening it the last thing the night before, when he was asking me for the key of the field-gate, as he should want to go out early. Surely, I thought, he can't have been past before I was up—before five o'clock! That seemed hardly likely. As I couldn't get into the house yet, I was obliged to keep the pocket-book in my hand a while; and keeping it in my hand made me mix up Mr. James with my thoughts about Martin.

Now, after I had sat there for about half an hour, I felt stiff, and got up to take a walk. I passed under the linden trees and over the grass towards the fields, thinking to myself that if Mr. James *had* gone to the village I might chance to see him coming back by this time.

The field-gate was a pretty sight any summer's morning about that time, when the fat cows all came crowding there, lowing to be milked; and the tall trees meeting over it were shaking themselves awake; and you could see the heat of the day come rolling up in a white mist over the little copses and the long wet fields. Ay, it was a pretty sight; and while I stood looking at it this morning, glad of the warm breath of the cows on my hands, though it was August, I saw two figures standing at the edge of Dyer's Dingle that didn't seem at all out of place in the picture. At first I thought it was the dairy-woman Dorcas and our young Phil Hind; but by-and-by I made out clear as a pike-staff that he I took for Phil was no other than Mr. James,—ay, our plodding Mr. James, and talking to a woman too! Just as I was wondering if the woman was really Dorcas, I heard the swing of a pail behind me, and there was Dorcas running along blithe as a bird, just come out of the house.

When she opened the gate with a flounce, because I wasn't Phil Hind, I suppose, I took my way out of it and across the field towards the dingle, with Mr. James's pocket-book.

Before I got half way, he parted from the woman, and came homewards across the grass, plodding along with his hands behind him and his head a little forwards, just as usual. What in the world possessed me, I don't know, but I actually let him pass me without turning off the footpath to meet him and give him the pocket-book; and so I found myself jogging along as

fast as ever I could go to the edge of the dingle.
When I got there and looked down, there was
Mr. James's companion sitting on the ground,
smoking a little black pipe, and counting some
silver in her hand.

She was a gipsy woman, about fifty or sixty
years old I should say, hard and brown as a
penny.

I went back without her having seen me, and
walked fast to overtake Mr. James before he
should go into the house. This was all ominous
enough to make my Mistress Pole turn in her
grave. Before five, such an unheard-of thing as
Mr. James dropping his pocket-book happens;
and then, before six, I see a gipsy, a stone's
throw from the house, talking to somebody living
at the house,—living indeed almost in Martin's
own room !

When I overtook Mr. James, he was in the
hall unbuttoning his gaiters.

"You've dropped your book, sir," I said.

He gave a slight start, and looked at the book,
and felt outside his pocket as if he couldn't

credit it, and then taking it from me, quietly said,

"This is a very odd thing, Matthew; it never happened me before; no, to my recollection, never. There is a shilling. You won't take it? It is reward enough for you to have been so fortunate as to find it; I know it is; thank you, Matthew, thank you!"

"How is the Squire, sir, this morning, if you've seen him?" said I.

Mr. James shook his head and gave a sigh.

"If you please, I should like to see the Squire," I said, taking a step further into the hall.

"My good man," said Mr. James, "I wish the Squire *would* see you or any one, but he won't, he won't; and we mustn't cross him. Ah, Matthew, my man, I wish this day were over."

Mr. James took his handkerchief out and turned away. I went and got my breakfast; but my early walk to the dingle had not given me an appetite, whatever Mr. James's might have done for him.

If I were to be hanged for it, I couldn't say what I did that morning from seven till eleven; I only know those four hours were the longest I ever lived through. I've some recollection of muddling about in the peach-wall walk, and carrying my eye incessantly from Martin's window to the dingle, and from the dingle to Martin's window; but that's all, till a servant came to say Mr. James wanted to see me.

As I wanted to see him, I was glad of the message; and made haste to change my coat and show myself at his private room, which was on the second story, had an iron-plated door, and was fitted up as an office.

"Come in, Matthew," he said; "seat yourself, seat yourself."

And I went in, but didn't seat myself, but stood watching him as he turned over the papers in the letter-bag which had just been brought up to him.

"Matthew," said he presently, turning to me and rubbing his hands round slowly, and speaking in a kind of troubled whisper, "Matthew, we are going on sadly down stairs; ve-ry, ve-ry sadly! This will be a trying day; to me a particularly trying day."

"Do you mean, sir," said I, "that the Squire is so bad?"

Mr. James sighed and shook his head, as much as to say, nobody but himself knew *how* bad.

"The truth is, Matthew," he said, "we're in a wrong state of things; but he mustn't be crossed; no, he mustn't be crossed. This is wrong—particularly wrong, I consider it—this that he insists on doing now; but I will not, to save myself pain, cross him in it; no, I will not have him crossed. Matthew, my brother desires you, as his most confidential servant, to go over to his lawyer, Mr. Richard Ferrers, at Bodington, and say that, owing to the very precarious state of his health just now, he is feeling exceedingly anxious about his will; and, as he is now of age, would be glad to see Mr. Ferrers as early in the day as he can possibly come."

I looked at Mr. James, and he looked at me. It must have been a particularly trying state of things for him certainly; when I knew as well as he did, that making a will at all, meant settling everything on himself, instead of leaving the property to go back to those who would have had it if old Squire Pole had never married a second time. Yes, it was a very trying state of things for Mr. James; and I think he read my thoughts, though he kept the same steady look as if my face were nothing but a row of figures, and presently said—

"Do you understand, Matthew? will you put it to Mr. Ferrers in this way?"

I stood about half a minute considering, then stepped up and laid my hand on his desk, and said—

"I beg your pardon, sir; but I should like to have a word with the Squire myself before I go."

Mr. James was rather hard of hearing sometimes; he put his hand to his ear now, and said—

"Eh?"

"I want to see the Squire, sir;" and I took care to speak pretty loud.

He considered a moment, but I think he felt I was not going to be put off this time, for he rose, taking up the letter-bag, and said to me—

"Well, well, I don't know; I don't like to cross him, but he really ought to see you on this matter; it would be better, wouldn't it, to take Mr. Ferrers a message from himself? Come, then, Matthew, come; and I'll try and prevail on him to speak to you."

We went down stairs into the hall, and he opened the baize-covered door of the passage leading to Martin's rooms.

To my astonishment the inner door was locked, and Mr. James took the key from his pocket.

"What the —— Hem! pray, sir, what is the Squire locked in for?" said I. He gave me a wondering, sorrowful kind of look, and said—

"Do you forget what this day is, Matthew? How can we be too cautious? Remember his mother's dying injunctions. Hush, tread very quietly; please, hush-sh!"

At the door of the bed-chamber he pulled out another key, and I really began to think Mr.

James was more wrong in his head than Martin. He went in first, and then beckoned me, and put up his finger to warn me to be very quiet. At first I could scarcely see two inches before me. Not a single gleam of daylight came into the room. Martin's bed-chamber opened into another room, called the long-room, which had windows on the lawn, just in front of the fountain; but now the shutters were up and barred; and all there was to light the two great rooms was a single wax candle, standing on a cabinet beside the old time-piece.

By-and-by my eyes got used to it, and I made my way to the great bed at the far end of the chamber; and there, propped up with pillows, feverish-eyed, white as a ghost, and slimmer and smaller than he was at sixteen, I saw Martin Pole. He put his hand out to me and smiled.

"Sir, sir," I said, "this is a bad look-out."

"So you've come to see me at last, Matthew?"

"Yes, they wouldn't let me come before," I said; "but I would come and wish you many happy returns of the day, sir."

He shivered a little; and Mr. James screwed his face up, and gave me a severe shake of the head; then he came up on tiptoe to the bed and said to Martin—

"Matthew will not stay; he just came, because he thought it better for him to tell Ferrers he brought the message direct from you."

"Ah, yes," answered Martin, faintly; "tell him to come as soon as he can."

"But what's this will-making all about, sir," said I, "if I might take the liberty to ask? You don't look as you ought, to be sure, but it needn't come to will-making yet, that I can see."

"That will do, Matthew; you can go," he said, in a much stronger voice.

Mr. James rose from where he sat reading a letter, and went to open the door very politely; but I stood still where I was, looking at Martin Pole. Things were taking a shape I couldn't exactly make out, and didn't at all like. I thought of my picture over the field-gate; and, somehow, Mr. James's movements out of doors and his movements in doors didn't seem to me

at all to agree together. I was just going to
make some kind of mention of what I had seen
before them both, when, just as if he had read
my thoughts, Mr. James saved me the trouble.
He shut the door he had been holding open for
me, and, coming back on tiptoe to the foot of
the bed, said in a whisper, but loud enough for
me to hear—

"I was unsuccessful this morning: it was not
her. I found the woman I have had in my eye,
but it was not her. I am very sorry my plan
has failed, for I am sure it would have been the
best thing possible if you could only have talked
with her herself, and seen how little she really
thought of it after the time being."

Martin closed his eyes, and lay back with a
tired look; and again Mr. James opened the door
for me, and again I kept him waiting.

He had just cleared two dark suspicions off
my mind about the will, and about the gipsy;
and you would think I should have gone away
in peace, glad that Martin had such a brother
to watch over him; but the more I looked at

Martin the more certain I felt that all this watching and door-locking and darkness was just like pushing him to madness or death. Now did Mr. James know this, or was he nursing him to death out of pure brotherly kindness and innocence?

Here was the day on which some terrible death had been threatened for Martin before he was born, and which his whole nature had been filled with dread of. It had come, and there he lay in a hot room, with the daylight and the air shut out, and his eyes fixed incessantly on the clock, counting the seconds as a man who opened a vein might count the drops of blood that were taking his life away.

Did Mr. James know what he was doing, or did he not?

There he was holding the door open for me; and there was Martin Pole with his eyes on the clock; ay, and at that instant I saw him (though he thought I didn't) dabbling with his fingers on his pulse. It was only twelve at noon yet; what would he be if this went on till twelve

at night,—till the last second of the appointed
time?

I looked from one to the other for some little
while; Martin might have counted thirty seconds
in it perhaps, and then my mind was made up.

"Don't trouble yourself, Mr. James," said I,
"I'am not going just this minute, thank you!"
And then I went close to Martin, and made
bold to take up the noble, wasted, white hand
in my own, and I said to him—

"Mr. Martin Pole," I said, "you're a scholar,
and I'm not; now can you tell me this? Because
a man's a servant, and bound to obey his master,
must he be kept from doing his duty by him as a
fellow-man?"

"I don't understand you, Matthew," he said.

"Well, sir, this is what I mean. I know what
this day is as well as you. I know that, through
things you couldn't help, it must, taken any way,
be a heavy day for you to get through; but then,
sir, there are two ways of taking it, a right and a
wrong. Now I want to know if I'm at liberty to
say which it is I think you have taken?"

"Really, Matthew," said he, colouring a little, "I don't know who it is has given you to understand my illness has anything to do with this particular day; but as for being at liberty to speak your mind to me, you know you are so at all times."

"Thank you, sir," I said; "then I'll speak it in half a dozen words. You and Mr. James have taken decidedly the wrong way; you couldn't have gone more wrong, sir."

"How?" he asked.

"Why, sir, if you'd allow me,—a servant that's been in your father's house ever since you were born,—if, sir, you'd allow me to act as chief gentleman o' the bedchamber five minutes, I'd show you."

He laughed, and giving my hand a shake, said—

"O, you are quite welcome to do that, Matthew."

"Do you really mean it, Mr. Martin, sir?" I asked. And he nodded, and looked at me a little curiously.

My word! I determined to make the most of
that five minutes. My coat was off in an instant,
and then down came the bars from the shutters,
back went the shutters, and open the windows
flew; and then, from his bed at the far end of
the inner room, Martin could once more look out
upon the green lawn and the flowers, and the
fountain leaping and dazzling in the August
sunshine; once more he could breathe the fresh
air and hear the blackbirds singing in the linden
trees.

Mr. James began to sneeze, looking at me
between whiles with a patient, condescending,
melancholy smile, as much as to say, "Ah, my
poor old man, don't you think I should have
done all that before if it was of any use?" The
sudden change, however, did what I wanted for
Martin: it took his eyes off the clock for a minute
or so, but they soon travelled there again.

"And now, sir," said I, as I put on my coat
quite in a perspiration, "now that my time is up
as chief gentleman o' the bedchamber, may I
have five minutes as doctor?"

"O yes,"—and he took his eyes from the clock to see what I was going to do. First I pretended to feel his pulse, then I said—

"I shall be about two hours going to Mr. Ferrers; now you must do something for that time to stop thinking about yourself, that's what I prescribe." He looked more like himself than he had done that morning, as he sat up in bed, and shook my hand with real heartiness.

"Matthew," he said, "you are right; I will try. James, we will," said he, looking at his brother.

"But how will you set about it?" said I. "It's as hard for some people to stop as it is for others to begin."

"If,"—said Mr. James, with a smile for his brother and a sneer for me,—"if *I* might be allowed to suggest to the learned doctor a way for carrying out his plan, I would advise that I read you this brown-paper-covered manuscript which came in the post-bag this morning. It is from some poor author who knew you at college, and who wants you to read it that you may, if

you like it, help him to a publisher, or to get up
some subscriptions for the book to tempt some
publisher to buy it."

"That will do," said I. "And now Mr. Martin,
sir, as your only medical adviser for the time
being, I command you not to interrupt Mr.
James till the story is finished."

He promised, and Mr. James, caught in his
trap,—for I'll never believe he wanted to do anything more than disgust Martin with the sight of
the bulky bundle of manuscript,—sat down by the
bed and began. So he was safely occupied. That
was something. Then I waited till the tale in-
terested Martin enough to draw his eyes from the
clock, and I began to feel pretty sure that he
wouldn't allow Mr. James to stop, even if that
gentleman should propose to do so. Besides, you
must remember that in any case Mr. James
would want things to go smoothly till after the
will was signed. Seeing things in this state I
slipped out to make preparations for the rest of
the day, while Mr. James went on with the
Plague-Stone of Aberford.

PLAGUE-STONE OF ABERFORD.

CHAPTER I.

LIFTING THE CURTAIN.

THE fire-light shines full on her face. The child feels instinctively that she must repress the faintest tremble of the lash, the slightest quiver of the nostril, the least movement that may betoken she is conscious of being secretly watched. Again and again has she, in her half sleep, half reverie, fancied there were eyes directed upon her through the little glass window of the door to the shop; and again and again has she pushed the fancy hastily and nervously away; but this time there could be no possibility of mistake; she had heard the soft approaching footstep, noticed the slow, careful rise of the corner of the curtain, and its remaining lifted, while a searching gaze, which she could not see, but which she trembled to feel, was watching her —she was sure of it!—in order to learn, perhaps, if she were asleep. Why? She cannot tell—she cannot even think just now, or speculate in any way, though her imagination is painfully active. The fact, by its mere existence, awes and absorbs her whole being. Half-remembered tales of women, placed in a position like this, when their very lives depended upon their strength and courage in enabling them to retain the appearance of sleep, rush in upon her, and confuse her with she knows not what dim suggestions of a corresponding necessity. If she be watched, who can be the watcher? Who but her father? He is the only person in the house, she believes, besides herself. If he it is, what can he meditate that——

But the child stopped suddenly in her thoughts, tightening, by a wild grasp of the reins of her soul, the half-frenzied alarms that were hurrying her away, she knew not whither; and she bent all her resolution to the task of preserving, under that mysterious gaze, a state of perfect quietude.

She heard the grey linnet flying to and fro in his narrow cage; she heard the mouse making a rustle among the heaps of books and pamphlets piled up at the far end of the room; she heard the fire crackling and burning cheerily; and thus alone she was conscious how the time was passing; while her face was growing paler and more rigid, her breathing faster and more laboured, under the influence of this long-protracted, secret examination. Once she was about to cry out, as in a dream, and she felt the very words struggling at her dry lips before she could overmaster them. She would have given worlds, if worlds had been in her possession, to have seen the fire-blaze droop and die. But, on the contrary, it leaped, and laughed, and babbled in its mirth with a kind of impish malice that curdled the child's blood, as she knew how its light was revealing her, and would not let her melt, like the other objects in the place, into shadowy indistinctness and rest—blessed, blessed rest! So there she still sat; and the vivid fire-light brought out all the sharp, angular lines of her form, and the childish and scanty cut of her clothes, which made her look so tall and gaunt, and gave her such a wild, overgrown air. But, above all, the ruddy, boisterous light seemed to seek out and illumine her small face, so youthful in its outline, yet so stamped with a foretaste of age that one almost expected to see grey hair about it, rather than that deep, close mass of blackness, brought to the shape of the head, like a cap, by being tucked behind the ears, and having the ends cut short.

Will that curtain never drop? Already the linnet, weary of pecking uselessly at the bars of the cage, is asleep on its perch; the mouse has scuffled away to her home behind the wainscot; and the Dutch clock gives warning that it is approaching the hour, and is about to strike.

The child's resolution falters; she can no longer

control the shrinking, straining nerves; the nostrils *will* quiver; the firm but sad mouth will twitch at the corners; the choking feeling will rise in the throat; a gasp—yes, she cannot help it—a gasp escapes her, and, on the instant, the little curtain falls! Oh, what a long, blessed sigh of relief the child gives!

Could it really have been her father? Was she still believed to be asleep, and, if not—— Again she checks, with a vague sense of their wickedness, the fancies that crowd all about her. She will not again be so spell-bound; she will resist in time. She starts up, stretches her aching limbs, and begins hurriedly to spread a cloth on the table, and to prepare a scanty supper for two persons, tutoring herself the while as to what she shall say when she goes to her father, who remains noiselessly occupied in the shop. Presently she walks to the door, touches the handle, feels it tremble, and—as she fancies—let go. She shivers inwardly, hesitates, goes back to the fire, gives it a plunging stir, sweeps up the ashes she has thus caused to fall, and then again suddenly grasps the handle of the door with a quick, nervous jerk, as though to give previous warning by the noise; but it so happens that she makes no noise. She then slowly opens the door, and looks in upon the darkened shop.

The gas has been put out long ago. The gloomy February night sheds no radiance over the tops of the closed shutters—does not even reveal, as usual, the narrow strip of sky. A candle, in a high lantern on the counter, throws a dim, uncertain gleam over the place; and it is some time before her eyes, just withdrawn from the intense red glow of the fire, can distinguish one object from another in the prevailing confusion. But she thinks only of her father, for it is him she seeks. She sees him stooping in the middle of the shop, between the heap of books and stationery that are piled high on each side of him, against the two counters. He is pouring something from one of the workmen's cans upon a heap of shavings left by the joiners, who have been altering the shelves.

"Father!" the child said, timidly, and scared at the sound of her own voice. It was a very sweet and childlike voice, but did not seem at all to belong to the wan, old-looking face. He started, dropped his arm with the can behind his back, but immediately—moved by a second impulse — brought it forward, and smiled. A strangely sweet smile the child thought it, as again she spoke—"Father, supper's ready."

"Oh, yes; I'll come. How you startled me, Constance! What careless workmen these are, to leave so many shavings about! I have been pouring some water over them for safety. Always guard against fire, my dear."

"Yes, father; I've been reading that book you left on the table to-night, that tells you what to do in case of fire, and what the chief causes of fire are, and all that—but, father, what is it smells so?"

"Oh, it's the empty turpentine-can I've been using to get water in."

"Father, hadn't I better take the shavings away?"

"No, no, run along—I'm coming. I'll just put them under the counter. They'll be safe there—sparks can't drop among them."

He went away with the shavings, and shortly returned, observing, quite cheerily—

"There!—now, Constance, for supper. I am tired with covering up books and things, but the plasterers, you know, are coming at six in the morning." So saying, Mr. Daniel Chorley took his daughter's hand, and they both went into the sitting-room.

A robust, fresh-coloured, genial-looking old gentleman he seemed as he stood by the fire in his soft, glossy, black clothes, frilled shirt, and silvery hair, warming, now his fingers, now his toes, and looking smilingly around, at first on things in general, then at his supper, then at Constance, who began to bask, though tremulously, in these rare but golden beams of a sunshine to which she had been little accustomed.

There was a curious resemblance, and a still more curious dissimilarity, between the two: he so healthy-looking, cosy, and prosperous; she so lanky, shabby, and sad; yet both alike in feature; and both exhibiting the same self-wrapped, secretive manner. In her this seemed to spring from timidity—the chill of a loveless life, and a shrinking from any—the least—demand for sympathy; not because it was not wanted, and would not have been esteemed as precious, but because the poor little heart had often ventured forth to seek something of the kind, and generally returned more sorrowful and hopeless for its vain quest. But it was nothing of this nature, certainly, that made the father so secretive beneath all the jovial expansion of his spirits. He was evidently a man who maintained a robust faith in himself. No wonder, when he saw how few other men there were who had not also the same belief in his abilities, character, and gentlemanly ways. That high, bare, glossy forehead seemed an open tablet, on which the world might read the nobleness and all-sufficiency of the deep, rich volume inscribed within. Yet to those who looked more curiously there appeared a sort of tight drawing of the skin from the crown of the head, and a faint crossing and re-crossing of wrinkles over the brow, as though produced by a kind of scarcely noticeable, but not the less real and unchanging, frown. There was also a restless and a furtive play of the dark eyes, which could never fix on anything, least of all on another human eye, and yet which could not rest in peace beneath their shaggy covert, but always seemed beating about and about some secret mental difficulty, but never daring directly to cope with it. Was he suspicious? Surely not—this cosy-looking, comfortable bookseller, whom his neighbours called, in genuine respect, "The old gentleman."

"There, child," he said, "put away your work, and sit down and enjoy your supper. Take a bit of this nice pie. Oh, don't be afraid, for once; besides, there's plenty for me."

The child looked, that she might make quite sure he was speaking seriously, then obeyed him, with a hesitating manner, and presently began to swallow—something more than the pie.

"Why, Constance, I declare your clothes are

all worn out—and—and—yes, quite shabby! Ah, well, we'll see to them soon, when trade revives. I must study appearances in the shop, you know, for myself, or you shouldn't have waited so long."

Did the child hear correctly? Her father talking thus to her—almost, she ventured to think, apologetically? He! who had never troubled himself before to give her even the commonest explanations? Her heart swelled; she thought she ought to say something. But she didn't know how to address him—and so she was silent.

"Here, Constance, child, come and sit by me. There now, give me a kiss. Pshaw! child, you have wetted all my face. There, there—bless the girl!—can't you be quiet? There! All's right now, isn't it?"

"Yes, father."

"If, now, we had only Marmaduke from school!"

"Ah, yes," replied the child; "he did so wish it."

"Yes, I know. Why, I wonder? Oh, I re-member; it is your birthday—so it is. Dear me! Why, how tall you grow for your age! Fifteen? No. Fourteen? Pshaw! Of course not—only thirteen. One fancies you much older, both from your body and mind. I ought to have remembered the year, I'm sure. Two such disappointments were enough to burn it into me—a fortune lost to the family, that was likely to have come to me—and——" But Mr. Chorley's speech rested there, with the unfinished sentence.

"What was the other disappointment, father?"

"Well, Constance, I'll tell you, because you are a sensible girl, and can understand my feelings. I expected a boy—a son and heir, you know—and, with my expectations just then——"

"O, yes, father—I'm sure I don't know why I came—I'm very sorry—I couldn't help it, father, you know, could I?—and—and——"

"Now, Constance, I hate crying—don't cry."

"No, father, I won't."

"There—there—that's a good girl!"

And Mr. Daniel Chorley put his arm caressingly round the little shrinking but yearning form, and brought her towards him, just a little; and she had a strange feeling, beforehand, of nestling at last in a father's bosom, and then— the bliss of that idea seemed too great to be ventured upon as a reality; and so she remembered that she had not drawn her father's beer, and she hurried away into a narrow closet between the parlour and the shop—"the lumber closet" they called it. There she put down her candlestick and jug, both very carefully; and the trembling knees bent, and the hands dropped on the cold brick floor, and the face dropped upon them, and the stout little heart gave way—oh, so sadly!—and the slender frame quivered under the force of the emotions that battled fiercely for the right to come forth to the sun and air. But the child struggled hard to quell the hysteric tide of grief before her father should overhear her, and destroy, in his just anger, all the fair hopes she was building up. Ah, yes, this might yet be a true birthday for her, she thought, if she didn't expect too much.

At last she rose, wiped her eyes in the lining of her skirt, drew the beer, and was hurrying forth in the fear that he would ask her why she had been so long, when her eye fell upon the pea-sticks, and the firewood, and the row of candles in bundles, and she looked round her uneasily, even while she said to herself—

"No, no—it's my wicked fancies! There's nothing here fresh but the candles—and he did buy just as many all at once, last winter."

But, in leaving the closet and shutting the door, the child could not help again opening it to take another long look, while saying to herself—

"I hope I left all safe."

When she returned with the jug to her father, he was evidently angry about the delay, yet he said little; and when he looked at her, poor Constance felt all the past revive, and there was no more thought that night of her nestling on a father's breast. The birthday dream vanished—for ever!

"Now, Constance, go to bed, and take care how

you put out the light. I will come up when I think you are asleep."

She rose to obey, but did not leave the room, and seemed to find one occupation after another to detain her.

" Constance, did you hear me ? "

" Yes, father, I am going. Good night."

" Good night."

And so they parted, as they had always parted before. No kiss exchanged—no pleasant thoughts to gild the entrance-gate to sleep—no loving fondness to make either feel they would be missed by the other, on the coming morn, if death should refuse to allow the lids to be opened that sleep had closed.

Scarcely, however, had the child reached the landing at the top of the stairs on the first story before her excited imagination was again at work, bringing more and more tangibly before her some vague dread of fire. It was strange—it was inexplicable—but it was to her, also, appallingly clear that there was scarcely a yard of the house or staircase on or about which did not hang the most dangerous things, if a fire should, by any accident, break out. She had just noticed the dry pea-sticks, firewood, and candles, in the lumber-closet. She remembered that in the shop the front of the book-shelves was protected all the way round by old curtains, or by sheets of paper, pinned end to end; that the counter was covered with books, and paper, and writing-desks, and things of that kind; and that they also were protected by the large sheets of brown paper that had been carefully placed over them by her father, before the plasterers began their work of whitewashing the ceiling. And, as she gazed about her on the landing, she saw a roll of paper about to be hung on the wall, partly unrolled and the loose piece hanging over the banisters, just as her father had left it after looking at the pattern. Other large rolls of old brown paper, received with parcels in the business, and carefully stored for future use, lay about, covered thickly with dust; also a great worn-out screen, on which, in its better days, Constance had gazed for hours together, on first waking in the summer mornings, and let loose her fancy with the birds that were gaily sporting all over it. It was tattered now, and strips of the surface were hanging loose. Old packing-cases, too, were on the landing, brought forth from the corners and recesses where they were usually placed in order to allow the workmen to go on with the renovation of the house. As Constance's mind ran rapidly over these dangerous elements of their home, it seemed to grow more excited at each step, until even the most insignificant facts assumed unnatural proportions, and she grew sick and wild with terror at the phantasms she had herself half created.

Just then there was a knock at the street-door. Constance knew the knock—it was that of their neighbour, Mr. Fleck, who usually came once a week or so to play a game of cribbage with her father. What did he want now? She listened. Her father opened the door, greeted Mr. Fleck with his usual cordiality, and brought him in. She must go to bed, she said to herself; but she did not go, for all that. There was a sort of fever

in her blood.   She seemed almost to want excitement now as food; she must listen, in the absence
of anything else to occupy her attention.   She
went to her room, on the second or top story, put
her candle on the little black box that contained
her worldly treasures, and slipped out again,
shutting the door after her to conceal the light.
As she noiselessly descended the stairs, she heard
that, instead of sitting down to cards, her father
was taking Mr. Fleck into the shop to see the
alterations; and at once, by virtue of that single
fact, the scales seemed to fall from the poor child's
eyes, and again she shrunk in horror from herself,
and from the thoughts that had darkly glanced
across her vision, but to which she had not dared
to give form or name.   She was about to run up
to bed, and pray to God to make her deserve the
peace that had fallen upon her, on knowing that
her father was showing all the place to their
rich and respected neighbour, when she heard
a stumble, and guessed it was Mr. Fleck, who
was near-sighted, and not very strong upon his
legs.

"No harm, no harm, Chorley," she heard him say; "I only stumbled over the can."

"Oh! it's the painters' turpentine, careless rascals! Dear me! it's running all over the floor, and will get into the books. Just hold them up while I find something to prevent the stream from spreading." Constance listened, while Mr. Fleck held up the books, and Mr. Daniel Chorley, bustling round the counter, fetched out a large handful of shavings, saying, "These will do capitally!" And she heard her father wipe up the spilt turpentine by the aid of the shavings. "Thank you," he continued; "that will do. The books are safe, and I'll put these shavings away in the lumber-closet, and they'll be safe too!"

"What a dismal light you have there, Chorley!"

"Oh, yes—the lantern. Why, you see, I'm afraid to trust myself here with an open candle, after dark, amid all this confusion. Would to Heaven I could get rid of these workmen! They keep me wretchedly nervous. I found to-night two or three lucifer-matches on the floor, dropped by them, I have no doubt."

" Ah, neighbour, you're not the man to have a fire in your house : a more careful person I never saw. But I hope you're insured, for all that ? *I* am, and I always sleep peaceably in consequence."

" Yes, I am insured. But it isn't the property — bad as it would be to have the worry of replacing it—no, it's the danger—the danger, neighbour—that most troubles me. Excuse me for one moment; I think I saw another of those infernal matches beneath your foot. No, no; 'tis nothing."

" Well, Chorley, I'm sure I hope you'll be repaid for all your trouble and expense in making these improvements. I think you will. And as one railway, at a distance, took the trade from our town, so this new one, that comes close, and which will open next week, may bring it back."

" That's just what I'm reckoning on. Oh! I wouldn't have gone to all this expense and worry, but that I saw a new era dawning—a new era, mark my words, sir—for this place, and for all its inhabitants."

" So be it.   Good night, Chorley."

" Good night, Mr. Fleck.   Thank you for coming in.   Then I shall expect you to-morrow, and early ? "

" Yes—at half-past eight."

" Good night ! "

The street-door opened and closed again, the bolts were drawn, the key was turned in the lock, and the child felt as though the whole world was being shut out, and that she ought to run to it for protection before it was too late.   She had heard the dialogue about the turpentine.   Oh ! what had her father been doing—and intending —when she had come upon him, bent over the shavings?   It was turpentine and not water that he had been sprinkling over them.   And why did he so deceive her ?   The ghastly fear *would* now be gazed upon and questioned—would not any longer be thrust aside.   The child felt all her senses grow benumbed.   Her trembling knees refused support, and she was obliged to clutch the banister to keep herself from falling. But she sees his light returning through the shop. Dare she confront him? Yes, she will; and the cry of "Father, what is this? oh, what are you doing?" is on her lips; but the well-known footsteps seem to bring reproach as they fall upon her ear. Her fear seems to melt to a mere fancy as the familiar sounds get nearer and nearer, until she thinks she can endure anything rather than that he should see her suspicion; and she seems to fly with winged feet up the narrow, steep stairs never once pausing till she stands, panting for breath, in her own room.

Presently she tries to undress, but her fear, which she had wrestled with and driven off, has not been altogether driven away. It returns, arrests her fingers, makes her gaze and gaze upon it, till she becomes fascinated by its awful form and flaming eyes.

In vain she thrusts at it with all her little strength, as though it were something corporeal, crying, "I won't believe it—I won't! I won't!" It stands immovable before her aching eyeballs, refusing to be disowned. Child as she is, this horrible spectre calls her parent.

Hark! Hastily she puts out her candle, and crouches down upon the bed, listening. She hears smothered, cautious footsteps—that would be noiseless but for the occasional creak of an old board—approach, and pause at her door. Now all is quiet again — so quiet, that she can hear a great moth knocking its wings about between the window and the blind. Hark! Again a board creaks, and this time at some distance from her door—then on one stair after another, and each time sounding more faintly. Yes, he has gone down. Whither?—what to do? She is standing in the middle of the room, gazing round, with clasped hands and wild, questioning eyes, as if the bare white walls might answer her. She opens her door noiselessly, goes out upon the landing, and stands looking down over the banisters into the unshapeable but almost living darkness. All is still. The wind outside seems to make the silence within more intense. A great lean cat, as it runs along the parapet, looks in at the broken window, leaps down, and comes and rubs itself against her legs with a loud, cheering purr. Very sweet to the lonely child is this touch of sympathy, and she cowers down lower and lower towards it, until she is sitting on the floor, with her arms folded round her knees, and the cat curling itself up for warmth on a bit of her frock. The child seems to find a sort of dreary comfort in that dark, dismal landing, and strange companionship. Then comes the wind, wilder than ever, whistling about the house-top, filling her ears with indescribable sounds, that she imagines to come, first from one part of the house, and then another. She even fancies she hears, as in a dream, or as a matter that doesn't concern her, the voice of her little brother, crying to her, as though he needed her, "Constance! Constance!" But nothing surprises her now. She only wonders if God ever goes away for a time, to see how the world will manage in his absence.

And now the cat rises, and turns restlessly round and round, and looks through the banister with an uneasy moan; and the child shivers to see her strange dread shared by another living thing besides herself. Now the wind sinks to rest, leaving a dead, unearthly stillness behind, upon which she is fearful of letting out her own breath, lest it awaken some other sound. The cat purrs again soothingly, and weariness creeps over the girl. Her eyes grow heavy—her head droops; but she suddenly starts up, only just able to prevent a scream at some fearful image that has passed before her closed eyes.

Some new thought quickens the beats of her heart, and warms the blood in her veins. She rises, and once more looks down those impenetrably black stairs. She will break the spell herself. Yes, she will go to her father, and tell him all that has been in her mind this wretched night. It can't be true! How can he forgive her if it isn't? Perhaps he may pity her a little for what she has suffered, and speak a kind word, or pass his hand over her head. Or, if he does not, but is only angry, as most likely he will be, the sound of his voice will comfort her, and her fear will be gone. She does not wait for the voice within her to supply another word, but glides down the stairs, running swiftly, as if she fears that something may happen to shake her resolution, or to interfere with it, before she gains his room. The door stands a little way open; she reaches his bed without having made the slightest noise. The room is in perfect darkness, so that she cannot see his face, but she stands there, listening eagerly to his breathing; it is sonorous and perfectly regular. Would he be sleeping here thus peacefully, if— Each breath swells the remorse in the child's heart till it becomes unbearable. Her lips and eyelids quiver like leaves before rain. Then comes a rush of tears, and a bursting, impetuous cry that will not be thrust back —

"Father!"

He rises slowly up, yawning, leaning on his elbow, and rubbing his eyes.

"Is it you, Constance? Why, what's the matter?"

The child presses close to him, and begins to

pour out all her pent-up anguish in tears and broken words—her voice now sinking to a frightened whisper, or changing into sobs, and now rising so loud and thrilling, that the listener, at first so calmly alarmed, stretches forth his hand with an angry and excited, " Hush ! "

" Father ! father ! I have been so wicked. Let me tell you all, for I am afraid to go to bed without. Don't be angry, father ; but I thought you were going to do something dreadful—so very dreadful, I can't say what—but it made my flesh creep to see you going about it all the evening ; and I dared not go to bed, but sat shivering on the landing, looking down in the dark, waiting and waiting for the end to come ; and when I nearly fell asleep, I thought I saw such things— oh, such fearful things !—great, high flames of fire, father ! red, roaring fire ! "

Again the hand was stretched out even more excitedly than before.

" Hush, girl, hush ! you shall talk no more like this. Listen. Constance, you are right ; you have been wicked ; and it would be a judgment upon you if a fire were to break out this very night ! ”

" Oh, father! don't talk so—don't—don't! ”

" Then go to bed, and have done with these wicked fancies. I'll go and look over the house to satisfy you, if you like."

He got out of bed, and stood before her half dressed, though the child did not notice the circumstance. As he put on a dressing-gown, he continued—

" What is it? Are you frightened to go alone? Then stay here till I come back."

But her hands closed more and more tightly on his arm, her head is thrown back, and her eyes fixed wildly on his face. He tries to speak calmly and kindly to her, but the drops stand thick upon his brow.

" Constance ! sit down child; your fancies have made you quite ill. Poor child! sit down. You're as white as a sheet ! ”

Again that hoarse, unnatural whisper thrills him—

" Father ! what is this ? It is black night

outside! There is no candle! How can you see my face? How can I see yours? Tell me, O father! tell me! what makes the room so light —light, red light, all over it?" Then, wringing her hands, she rushes distractedly about, crying, " What is it? oh, what is it? Father! father! father!"

As she turns to him again he clutches her shoulder, and mutters, with a faint, hollow voice, " I—I'm afraid there is a fire somewhere. I'll see. But hark! what—what was that?" And his own voice grew fainter than the one he listened to.

" What'! Why, it is they that are come— the great, high flames, father, you made! You did! you did! I watched you nursing them so that they might grow and grow right to the top of the house!"

" Con—stance!"

" Hush, I say!—listen! O God! there is something else!"

Yes, there is a strange sound penetrating through the angry roar—a faint, childish voice—

" Con—stance !   Con—stance ! "

The girl contracts with misery.   " Oh, father, father ! 'Duke must be here—in his bedroom. He must have come home without telling us, and climbed in at the back kitchen window, as he used to do, and so got up-stairs.   He asked me if he might, and I told him, No.   Oh, father ! father ! "

The father is staggering against the bedpost, and the words that issue from his pallid lips take the last thin veil from his act—" Oh, my God ! my God ! what have I done ? "

Again feebly and falteringly is the cry heard—

" Con—stance ! "

The red light that now displays every wrinkle, every line of remorse in the old man's face, suddenly becomes of a lightning-paleness in colour. Near the ceiling, a square flap of the canvas partition—it is a very old house, and strangely altered and patched—has fallen slowly back, and a cutting stream of white light enters, illuminating the floating particles of dust that it encounters in its way.

" Constance ! " This time the cry was sharp and piercing.

" Marmaduke ! Save him—save us, Constance ! "

The old man is stricken helpless; and, for the moment, the child can only run hither and thither, wringing her hands, and throwing them wildly up and down in the air, as she moans—

" Oh, what shall I do? what shall I do? Mother! mother! come back from Heaven and help me ! "

CHAPTER II.

YES, it had come—in a more awful aspect than even that in which her imagination had painted it. The fire had come!

The child—standing there with the full sense of her position, the flames before her, her father's guilt acknowledged, himself helpless and despairing, her little brother's cry ringing in her ears—felt, for an instant, her soul give way to the madness it had been so long struggling against. It was not in prayer she made that wild appeal for help to her dead mother—no, it was her soul rising within her, passionately resisting the cruel hand that had fallen so heavily—too heavily for her child's strength to bear. Then, as if that piercing cry had rent its way through heaven's gate, letting thence a breath of pure air issue, she felt a sudden calm playing like a cool breeze around her heated brow—it drove off the madness, and left her strong for thought and action.

"'Duke! 'Duke! I'm coming!"

The boy's cries for help cease. He has heard her. The old man, as he leans on the bed, paralysed mind and body by the awful consequence of his crime, is suddenly startled to his senses and his feet by that loud, clear, ringing, childish shout—a shout that, in its shrill treble, rises high above the deafening roar like a challenge from a power mighty as the raging fire itself—sent by God into that small body to combat with and quell it. And the trembling man obeys that voice which calls him to take arms against himself; and soon he is running hither and thither at her word, and watching for every gesture of her hand as his destiny.

There is not even pain in her voice now. The almost cheerful tone is not forced. Relief in action has come to her as to all brave souls : fearful enough—but still relief. No longer has she to struggle with a nameless, creeping terror— no, she sees now a living enemy to grapple with, hand to hand, to whom she can give war-cry for war-cry.

From the end of the long landing where they are, the flames come leaping towards them, catching at the torn paper of the wall and the loose heaps of pamphlets. It is but the work of a few minutes to unrol a lot of damp, mouldy carpet, throw it down, and stifle the flames under it. Then they clear the landing, as far as it is safe to venture, from the books and rolls of paper by throwing them out of the window into the little back-yard.

The breeze from the open window drives back the smoke and flame, and enables them to bear the stifling, pungent atmosphere, and to work; but it also feeds the fire. They see that, and they shut the window, but are compelled instantly to re-open it. They cannot live else: even with that help it is difficult to breathe. But through the thick, suffocating, yellow vapour, thus partially drawn aside, they perceive, between them and the child's door, a seething and crackling gulf of fire right through the flooring. Directly under that spot is the lumber closet, and the miserable father knows the fire has been too well laid there to be soon quenched by their feeble efforts.

But some new current of air drives the smoke along on one side of the landing, and up the stairs to the attics. A door has been opened; Constance catches a glimpse of a little white figure standing in the opposite doorway, and the sight stimulates her fast-failing strength, and rouses her from the almost irresistible pressure of despair that the first glimpse of that fiery gulf produced.

" We are coming, darling! keep back! we are coming!"

The father, though he never ceased working at her word or gesture, felt his own efforts weak beside hers. They had changed characters—he was the child, she the man. Hale and hearty though he was, he had never used himself to hard work; while Constance, whose strength had never been dissipated by luxury or idleness, had lifted his bales, and on dark winter mornings, when no

one could see (for Mr. Chorley would not have
liked that), had often taken down the heavy
shutters of the shop. From her straight figure
and upright walk the children of the town had
nicknamed her " the poplar," or the " little
poplar;" and to-night, as her lithe, agile body
swayed from side to side, avoiding the smoke and
flames as she worked, she seemed the very spirit
of that desolate, murmuring tree, as it turns to
lash the wind that frets it.

On they went—the child and the fire—now
both for a moment sinking exhausted, and then
at the least sign of returning strength in each
other, rushing again to the combat with redoubled
force. One minute she drives it before her,
smothering the flames as she goes with damp
carpet; at times, even with her feet and hands,
still striving to reach the side of the abyss, and
shouting every minute to the trembling boy with
a hopeful, ringing voice.

Another minute, and the fire bursts out afresh
on either side, compelling the boy to retreat and
shut the door against even his father and sister,

and forcing Constance herself back irresistibly—
nay, even licking her dress with tongues of flame.
But, snatching up her skirt, and rumpling it
suddenly with her fearless hands, she was able
to retreat in safety—sick, breathless, and exhausted.

"Father, water! Quick! we must have water!"

He stirs not. A new horror has seized him.

"Father, make haste! What is it? You
don't mean that——?"

"There isn't any! I let it off!. Oh, Constance! what must we do?"

"Did you throw away the buckets I drew for
the wash?"

"No! where are they?—in the yard?"

"Yes! Oh, make haste, father! make haste,
or it will be too late!"

She saw him tremble at the double meaning
of those words, "too late," and a thrill of pity
for him went through her heart.

"Father!" she whispered, as his foot was on
the stairs, and as she drew fresh life from the
window, "let's work hard, and put everything

right again, and no one shall ever know how it began."

New hope and new terror (for, in the anguish and remorse produced by the sight of his son's danger, he had forgotten the possibility of his own discovery and punishment) quickened the father's feet, and he was back with the water before Constance thought he had unfastened the yard-door. But almost fatal had been the delay as it was. The heat, smoke, and noise increased. The boy's cries became fainter and hoarser from behind the door which he dared not open; and the old man grew more and more distracted and unfit to act, as he saw the growing impossibility of removing the obstacle he had raised between him and his darling. He could do nothing but watch helplessly from the stairs how the fire rushed on and up, with a roar of exultation. But that roar is answered. Again that tiny, shrill voice rings through the house, dauntless as ever—

"We are getting on, darling! Keep back till I come! Open the door when I tell you. Father, we can't put the fire out—I must go through it and fetch him! The screen—quick! the screen—from the top landing! We must make a bridge across. Perhaps it may shut out the fire for a minute!"

She cannot repress a shudder as she watches the leaping and [quivering bursts of flame and smoke, and sees piece after piece of the reddened boards of the flooring drop inwards at the least touch, making the cavity still larger. But she profits now by her reading, of the evening before, in that book which her father had examined for a very different purpose.

While he fetches the screen, the child hurriedly soaks the blankets that they had previously fetched from the beds. She spreads two of them on the floor. She wraps another—the smallest—around her; she puts one aside for her father; and then empties the buckets on the carpets, which have hitherto helped to protect this part of the landing.

"Put that blanket on, father!" she cried, as he returned staggering under a great red screen. "That book says you don't catch fire so. Now help me to wrap these blankets round the screen.

And now, father, you keep that side, and help me
to push it along as far as you dare go."

But the old man can dare a great deal with
her now. Creeping along the floor on their hands
and knees (where they discover they breathe
more freely), they push the screen before them;
and they get nearer and nearer, though the
smoke is stifling, the heat terrible!

The screen approaches the gulf—it is pushed
across the edge, and they are conscious they are
shutting down the fire, inch by inch; and still,
with averted heads and panting breasts, they push
it on till it is nearly across, and they can bear no
more—not even though they know not whether
the end will catch on the opposite side as they let
it go. But no, it has *not* reached the cross-beam,
which is its only safe resting-place; the slight
flooring edge on which it caught crumbles away
with a thousand brilliant morsels scattered from
its burning side, as the end of the screen slips off
and begins to sink.

The old man wrings his hands in despair, and
then he crawls back, more dead than alive, to the

window, to get fresh breath from the wind that is pouring in; and the boy, as he crouches down on the other side of the door, listening to the preparations for his deliverance, hears the hiss of the dripping end of the blanket as it falls over from the sloping screen. But, in an instant, Constance plunges her hand unhesitatingly through the rotten canvas-work of the screen right into the fire; and, heedless of the torture, she grasps the framework and stays the frail bridge in its downward course. Once more it is raised, but her strength is not sufficient to push it more securely on to the beam.

"Father! father!" she screams hoarsely. He comes from the window again, and while she holds it up he pushes it safely on to the cross-rafter. O the grateful burst of the child's heart as she cries at last, "'Duke! 'Duke! Come!— you are safe!"

But there is no answer. She springs across the screen, pushes the door, but can see nothing within. Presently she feels something at her feet. The boy has fainted, but she

has him up in her arms instantly, and to the
window, which is a little open, and he revives
and tries to smile as he sees who looks upon
him.

O that face! O those eyes drowned in tears
of agony! They shine like liquid fire—they
burn and burn their beauty into the boy's soul,
until he grows self-forgetful, and falls to wondering whether God has already taken Constance for
Himself, and arrayed her in angel glory.

The frail bridge has to be re-crossed, and Constance is aware it will not bear them both at
once.

" Quick, darling ! keep to the wood in the centre!" she cries. "Father!—he is coming, father!"

" My boy ! " is almost upon the old man's lips.
But the black smoke, and the sickening odour of
the blankets, warn him, and he cries out, " Oh
God ! The fire will be through in a moment ! "

He had checked it by covering the hole Constance had made, but now the entire fabric was
fast going. He saw, and shouted—

" Quick ! give him to me, Constance ! Don't

you come yet. Hold him out as far as you can, and I'll take him."

It is done! The boy is safe—safe in his father's arms—but the screen bursts. In an instant Constance is driven back into the boy's bed-room —is compelled to shut the door—and she remains there, divided from father, brother, perhaps life itself, by a barrier which, though momentarily subdued, now springs up with irresistible fury, and follows her with mocking laughter.

But what is that to him—the father—who is out in the street—out in the pure, invigorating wind—trembling over his joy, like a robber over his lawless wealth?

" Constance—where's Constance? " are the first words on the boy's lips when he revives.

The father starts—*not* at the thought of what might now be her fate—no, though he would regret that, too, if he had more time, but that her name has roused in his mind a recollection of far more importance to him. He puts the boy down, saying—

" Yes, yes, call the neighbours. Have a ladder

put up to the window for her—but take care, my boy, for God's sake, take care of yourself, take great care! Mind, I forbid you to come into the house." As the little fellow ran off, his father muttered to himself, in a hollow voice, "Now, Daniel Chorley, save yourself, or you are ruined for ever! If you can't put out the fire, you must, at any cost, remove the traces of your own work."

And never did man more heroically brave fatigue, or pain, or danger, than did he now, while engaged in undoing the many and ingenious arrangements he had made for securing the prosperity of the fire.

With singed hair, once so white and silvery—blackened face—blistered hands—dry, burning lips—reddened, smarting eyes—bruised and bleeding limbs—he fought his way from point to point, and so at last into the shop, which he had calculated would have been the first to take fire from the closet, through its thin timber walls. But, in fact, the shop had only just now been touched, through the opening cracks of the woodwork.

He tore down the curtains and the suspended paper—some of it just as it was beginning to blaze—and he fearlessly trod out the flame; then, remembering the previous success up-stairs, he ran for a wet cloth, which he tried to hang against the breach the fire was making, but could not manage it; there was nothing to hang the cloth upon, and he was too nervous to invent a support. The smoke and the fire were also again driving him back, and overpowering him; but he pulled away the books from the adjoining shelves; and he swept, with frenzied hands, every-thing that might readily burn from off the counter; and then, as he saw a new fire spring up where he had left some smouldering paper, and which had been fanned by a freshly-en-tering breeze, he again rushed upon it, and was thus engaged, stamping upon it with an almost insane frenzy, when, to his inexpressible relief, he heard voices calling out cheerily to him—

"All right, neighbour—here's help. Leave it to us now. Come out—come!"

"Thank God! thank God!" devoutly murmured the sincerely-thankful man. "Oh, neighbours, save the property!—save the books! I
have done my utmost. Water!—I am perishing
with thirst! Give me some water!"

And while friendly hands fetched him a glass
of the most delicious nectar that ever passed
mortal lips, he had a vague consciousness of a
great crowd of men—some with water-buckets—
and of cries in the street, and of the rolling of the
wheels of approaching fire-engines, and of his
being led forth, with great interest and sympathy,
into a neighbour's house, and of some one saying
to him, "Pray be at ease, Mr. Chorley, there is
really no danger. We shall soon put down the
fire; you have nearly quenched it yourself!" and,
above all, of the exclamations and interchanges of
remarks—"The brave old gentleman!" "Did
you see how he was struggling with the fire?"
"Yes—yes." "He's insured, too!" All this he
was conscious of, in a dreamy kind of way; and
he was happy, for (and that was the only thought
he could now dwell on) he was safe!—his

character safe !—his crime unsuspected ! Who knows? perhaps he was even to benefit by the calamity! That thought wonderfully increased his recovery.

Not once, while his own future was thus at stake, had he recollected Constance—the brave, heroic child whose fortitude had alone inspired him with the hope or the strength to save the boy or his own reputation. But now her image rushed back upon him, and he started with no feigned alarm—

"The girl ! Constance ! Where is she?"

Two or three faces were around him; they looked from one to another, and answered in a condoling manner, which, had it been 'Duke they were speaking of, would have driven the father mad; but, as it was only Constance, he took their words as they were meant—kindly—consolingly.

"Don't be alarmed, Mr. Chorley. They've got the ladder up, but the window-sash was jammed fast, as though forced up in a great hurry by the poor thing, and there it stuck; but they have broken it away now, and are getting in. She

can't help them—but I daresay she's only fainted.
Take another glass of wine, neighbour, and don't
fear, they'll manage it.   That brave boy of yours
is safe with them."

Mr. Daniel Chorley turned his head away and
drank the wine, feeling as proud as if the praise
of his "brave boy" were his own personal
property.

CHAPTER III.

THE LITTLE POPLAR.

WHEN Constance found herself cut off from her father and brother by the fire—hemmed in and gazed on at every side by a fearful death—she felt all her sudden and preternatural strength forsake her, and became once more the helpless, frightened child. She stood a moment staring with wild eyes through the fire, to see if there was not a firm inch of the screen to rest her foot on if she dared to venture, but it curled up like paper, and fell bit from bit; and she turned sick with the noisome smell of the burning blankets; so she shut the door, and staggered back into the room. She clutched with desperate fingers at the slightly-open window; but, though it moved a little higher up, that was all it would do; it stuck fast there, and became only the more inextricably immovable from the frantic way in which the child strove to

· push it open wide enough for her to look out and see if she might leap down. Failing in the attempt on the window, she yielded utterly, and slid down upon the floor, not utterly senseless—better, far better, had she been so—but with just enough remaining consciousness to feel her fearful position to its fullest extent, without being able to battle against it.

The fire made great progress, and soon got into the chamber through the thin lath-and-plaster wall over the door; a beam across the ceiling of old, tindery wood, reaching from the door to the window, began to be wrapped about, through its whole length, with thin, darting, intermittent flames.

Constance, as she lay there directly under it, was only vaguely aware of the crackling of the dry wood, and of a vivid, blinding light, which made her long for any kind of darkness, even that of death; but she felt that she must die before the fire reached her. What with the aching of her limbs, the pain of her hands and feet, and the violent throbbing of her head, she felt that to live and be at ease again was impossible. She must die, and the faintness that was creeping over her seemed like the approach of death—and she tried to pray. But her mind wandered—not to the fire —she was hardly aware of its presence—but far back into the past—as minds will wander at such times, as though seeking for the other end of life to join to this, that they may hold up the finished circle to look at.

Minutes became hours as she lay there, blind to the light, deaf to the noise, in that twilight of death that was gathering in her mind. What the night would be when it came, whether it had moon or stars, she questioned not, but watched the shadows lengthening, and was still.

Now it seemed to her that she stood at her mother's death-bed, straining her ears to catch the last words. How distinctly she heard them *now!* —She repeated them over to herself, as she had done many and many a time before. " Constance, when your life is bitter to you, child, and you long for death, think of the little helpless charge I leave you, and live for him as I have lived for

you." The heart yearns to answer to that—
" Mother, I will ! I will ! " and the child tries to
move her limbs, but the sight of that burning
beam paralyses her ; the monster she has striven
with all the night has her in its power now, and
stands over her with a gigantic flaming sword,
hovering ready to drop on and crush her. She
might escape that sword had she but strength to
do and to will; but her mind seems lost in some
region between life and death, and not a sign to
guide it back.

But now she bursts out into wild, hysteric
laughter—what is it she sees? A face—a human
face ! Beautiful, O how beautiful, to the child,
because it is human ! Once more all her senses
rush back, just to let her pulses throb with life,
to let her ears drink in the exquisite music of a
human voice, to let her feel herself wrapped about
by strong human arms—and there they leave her.
And when again consciousness returned, it was in
a dull, heavy way, and she fell into a quiet, calm
sleep, from thorough exhaustion.

When she awoke she was herself again, and

could turn over in her mind all the events of the
night up to the time when her father parted from
her; but beyond that there was a blank. She
opened her eyes to see where it was she had been
laid down. And, without turning her head, she
could tell, by the pattern of the paper on the wall,
that she was in Mr. Fleck's parlour, and she knew
she must have been carried there from the fire.
She was going to give way to the sleep that was
again stealing over her, when she suddenly thought
of her father. Tears stole down her cheeks as she
remembered that perhaps, while she lay in that
sweet rest, he was hiding in some corner of the
street, a prey to remorse and grief; and then the
child sickened with terror at the new dread—
" Perhaps they have found him out, and taken
him to prison!"

She rose upon her aching arm, and looked
round. There stood Mr. Daniel Chorley, the
centre of an admiring group, relating eloquently
the breaking out and the progress of the fire. He
told of his alarm at the first discovery of the awful
fact; of his efforts and danger while saving his

children; and, as he drew towards the end, where his story grew more exciting, because it was more true, his cheeks glowed and his eyes flashed as he remembered that at this point, at least, he *was* the hero he described. Just then the agent of the insurance office, heated and alarmed, bustled in, and asked many rapid questions, and received from the bystanders earnest and enthusiastic replies; and he was so moved by the concurring testimonies, that he took off his hat and went to the old gentleman, and said—

" I must thank you, Mr. Chorley, in the name of the office, and before all present, for your courageous, admirable conduct."

And then there was a burst of applause, and people came up and shook the old gentleman by the hand, and said so many kind things to him, that he, who was at all times a susceptible man in anything concerning his own personal shame or glory, was quite overpowered with the sense of his nobleness, and he turned away with tears in his eyes.

He would not have turned that way at such a

moment had he thought of meeting the glance that awaited him—a glance which, mournful and stern as the eye of an accusing angel, stopped the course of those ignoble tears, and drove them back in shame to their base source.

The old gentleman's health had now to be drunk, and many more compliments were paid; but the child saw nothing more, heard nothing more, but turned her face to the wall, loathing life.

CHAPTER IV.

ONE evening Constance sat alone in the room behind the shop. She was looking at a map upon her knee, and now and then she concealed it beneath her work, and, leaning her head against the fire place, fell into deep, sad thoughtfulness.

Some weeks had passed, and wonderfully had Mr. Chorley recovered from the effects of the fire. The tide of fortune had come—somewhat differently, it must be owned, from what he had anticipated—but still it had come, and he was thankful—very thankful. His business had made a sudden leap forward, for every one took a pleasure in showing their sympathy with his misfortune, and their admiration of his courage, by coming to his shop to make some new purchase, or to give him some new order.

That afternoon the agent had been with his note-book, and looked at the damaged property. He happened to drop in at Mr. Chorley's tea hour, when the room was filled with the fragrance of the hot buttered cakes and the Mocha coffee, which were always irresistible to Mr. Rowbotham, and which Mr. Chorley, though he preferred tea himself, happened, quite accidentally—so he said—to have on the table that afternoon. It scarcely needed Mr. Chorley's persuasive voice to make him sit down and refresh himself before going to business. In the course of conversation, Mr. Chorley remarked that he had drawn up a careful estimate of the injured property for his own use; and Mr. Rowbotham, who disliked trouble, requested to see it, and, as he glanced it over, declared he would encroach no longer on Mr. Chorley's time by needlessly going over these items again. So business, without seeming to be business, was quickly grappled with, and soon over. It was not a case, Mr. Rowbotham felt, for rigid scrutiny into the exactitude of every particular of the loss, or into the precise amount attached to each item. Was it not plain that, but for the brave old gentleman's devotion and personal risk, the office must have had to pay three or four times the amount ? The agent felt it was not only absurd, but lowering to the dignity of the office and his own self-respect, to sit there chaffering with so estimable a man, so hospitable a host, and so old a customer. Accordingly, he accepted Mr. Chorley's estimate with entire good-will, and wrote beneath it, " I am satisfied this is correct, and that, if it be consistent with the views of the directors to make some additional acknowledgment of the zeal exhibited in saving the property in danger, this is eminently a case for their attention. It is impossible to speak too highly of the conduct of Mr. Daniel Chorley."

When he had written these lines he handed the paper over to that worthy gentleman, who read, and then wiped his eyes with a fine and snowy-white cambric handkerchief—another of Mr. Chorley's gentlemanly, but innocent, luxuries. After a while he said, in a mild, melancholy accent—

"The sum is—then—without the workmen's bills——"

"Fifty-nine pounds, ten shillings, and sixpence."

"Well, Mr. Rowbotham, I cannot exactly thank you, because your first duty is to your office; but I do say this—it is pleasant to have to deal with a gentleman. I say no more!"

At all events, he could have said nothing better to the purpose. The agent was a humbly-born, self-made man with a thriving income, and he was beginning to think of a lift in the social sphere, so that the idea of being esteemed a gentleman was peculiarly pleasant to him. The fumes of the fancy ascended into his brain, and wound about it with as pleasant a sense of titillation as the aroma of the coffee had already exercised upon its material structure.

"You are an honour to the town, sir—an honour to human nature!" were the agent's last words, as, two hours later, having finished his second tumbler of whisky-and-water, he shook hands with Mr. Chorley at the street-door.

But Mr. Chorley, though conscious of the existence of certain—(might he not say, practically slight?)—qualifications of the agent's opinion, was, on the whole, very much of the same mind himself. Were there not undreamed-of depths of virtue and conscientiousness in his bosom, known only to himself? No one but he, for instance, knew how easily he could have made those figures relative to the damaged property ascend considerably higher, yet he had refused to do so. He wanted to get rid of that cursed secret debt which had long weighed him down, and, having got the requisite amount in full, with a kind of gentlemanly allowance of a few pounds over, he would seek no more from the office—no, not even although he had, as the agent said, saved the office hundreds by his own personal risk and heroism. "Well, well, on the whole it was a happy ending—safer, yes, safer, than if everything had turned out as he had intended."

Yes, his only existing—and secret—difficulty was disposed of. A debt of fifty pounds had been pressing heavily on the old gentleman for some time, and of late had become so threatening that it had materially helped to influence the mind of the worried debtor to the dangerous course he had taken. But even that was now removed during Fortune's smiling, open-handed mood.

Of the conversation between the two men Constance had lost not a word.

Strangely stern, as well as mournful, had the pale face become now; though with little 'Duke it never lost the supernatural beauty he had seen come upon it in the smoke and flames of that horrible night. The few days he remained at home he seemed almost to idolise her. He followed her about from room to room. He looked up silently in her face, sometimes putting up his lips for a kiss when he saw a tear glistening in her eyes; and he never rested an hour away from her side. But Mr. Chorley sent him back to school, and the girl lost the bit of sunshine that his presence made upon her life.

And yet his absence was, in some measure, a relief—a great relief to-night, when she sat there, watching the shadow of another coming event, with very much the same kind of feeling that she had watched and foreseen during the night of the fire. But this time she was prepared—or, rather, trying to prepare herself—for a much harder battle than she had fought before, though, perhaps, 'Duke might not have understood it so.

She knew her time was come now; for she heard her father, who had busied himself in his accounts after the agent's departure, whistle a low, soft whistle, as he always did when he got up from his accounts satisfied. She rose, put the map in her pocket, folded up her work, and stood facing him as he entered the room, and said, in a firm, determined, yet rather husky voice—

"Father, I want to speak to you, please."

But at that moment Mr. Daniel Chorley remembered that he had a most interesting engagement out of doors to supper, and that he must run up-stairs to dress without an instant's loss of time. He was stopped by the piercing tones, successively increasing in intensity, that followed him—"Father! father! father!"

"Well, well! What a plague the child is! Now, then, Constance," he said, returning in an ill temper.

"Father, you told me that man was not going to pay you anything for the damage done by the fire."

"Of course not. *He* doesn't pay; it's the office which pays. You don't understand these things, Constance."

"Father, I'm afraid I do. You are to be paid, then, a great sum of money?"

"And if I am, what then? The office is willing."

"Does the office know, father, that you set fire to your own house?"

What a terrible power there is sometimes in the simplest words! I don't think anybody had ever yet seen Mr. Chorley in a genuine passion. He was too dignified, too gentlemanly. He might cut you with the keen razor of his sarcasm, and then pour into the wound the corrosive sublimate of his kindness, but all in a quiet, self-controlled way that made you respect the

appearances of the man, while you winced under
the reality of his torture. It was sad that a
child's words—and those the words of his own
child—should be the first to unsettle so desirable
a state of things. For a moment his face appeared
at the white heat of passion; then, as his knees
shook, and his eyes glanced quiveringly round to
see if there were any listeners, he started forwards,
dropped his two hands on the child's shoulders,
and pressed her neck convulsively between them,
until she screamed—

"Father! father! don't kill me!"

"Hush, I say—hush! Say those words again,
that you said just now, as long as you live,
and——"

The child saw in his eyes and face all that he
hesitated to say, and from that moment felt she
was alone in the world. To the dead mother
succeeded a worse than dead father! The child's
last earthly hope of a father's cherishing love
passed away; and there remained but the terror
of his presence, the fear of his fear, the sickening
consciousness of a secret existing between them

which forbade all hope of future mutual confidence. He, on his part, presently repented of his violence, and began to understand—very unwillingly, it must be owned—that here was a new difficulty to be faced, and one that he could not help, in his inmost soul, resenting that it should dare to be a difficulty to him. But he began to apologise—to soothe Constance's fears—to defend himself from the terrible *imputation* conveyed by her words. That was his phrase—"imputation." When ugly facts can't be resolved away into air we talk of them as imputations, and find comfort in the sound.

"Now sit down, child, and let me explain to you a bit."

"Yes, father."

"I have paid this office a good deal of money —more than the sum they are going to pay me in return."

"Yes, father," said the child, fancying, she knew not why, there must be something in that.

"When the trade was better, and the stock

larger, I insured for the right amount, and I didn't alter the amount when times grew worse and the stock less."

"No, father, I know—you told me once you didn't like the office to see that you were losing ground in the business."

"Pooh, nonsense! I never said anything of the kind—couldn't have said it! But you won't listen, Constance."

"Oh yes, father, I will, I will!" and the eyes were dropping big tears as this was said. But Mr. Chorley, communing with his own spirit, saw he was engaged in a hopeless task—that there was before him, in that little shabby child, an inexorable logician, before whom all his pleasant self-delusions dispersed into vacancy, and against whom, as they touched, all his worshipped idols were sure to be broken in pieces. So he said, in his grandest manner, and with a reproachful tone not common with him, and therefore only the more forcible—

"Constance, you do not listen to me with proper respect. You don't understand my actions.

In time you will. Wait, and be silent; you are but a child. Wait, I say, and be silent."

There was just the least touch of menace accompanying these last words. The child felt it, and shivered; but she had only two alternatives—that of softening him and bringing him to repentance, and another so bitter that she would not yet yield to it. Looking up into his darkening face, she cried—

"Father, you will not take this money—oh, dear, dear father, promise me you won't, and then I will never let anybody know that you——"

Here the shaking, warning hand was raised, and she paused.

"I must, Constance! Don't you see I must?"

"Why, father?"

"Because they would know I must have a motive if I refused—and there could be but one."

"Oh, father, tell them you did wrong, and you are sorry."

Mr. Chorley got up with a loud laugh—the idea was so ridiculous! Yet there was no mirth in the sound, or in his feelings as he paced up and down the room.

"Do, father, do!" pleaded the child's earnest voice. "They know how hard you worked to put out the fire. And I will tell them more, and then you'll never be afraid of people finding it out; and, oh, father, you won't always look upon me as you did just now."

"Constance, are you mad? Pray be quiet."

"Father, I cannot, I cannot. Tell them anything you like, but don't take this money. Say you don't want it."

"But I do want it. I shall be ruined without it. I owe it all."

"Then, father, let us go away to a fresh place. Oh, I will so work for you, and so—so—love you, father, if you will let me; and 'Duke shall be everything to you; and you needn't mind me at all."

"I tell you, in one word, it is impossible. Don't you know where I am going this evening?"

"No, father."

"Why, the neighbours have got up a supper for me by subscription among themselves on purpose to meet me, and to compliment me, and all that. Very kind of them, I'm sure. Would you have me ungrateful? You see, Constance, that everything now might be so nice and comfortable, if you wouldn't be so silly. Here's the trade improving, debts about to be paid, neighbours treating me with increased respect, I—I may say, honour—yet you want me to go and spoil everything, and say to the whole town— 'No, no, my dear friends, you are all wrong! I shan't take this money! I don't want this trade! I can't eat this supper!' Now I appeal to you, Constance, is it likely that anybody in his senses would do that?"

The child made no answer. She sank into a chair, and her arms dropped on one of its arms, and her head followed, and she forgot father, mother, world, everything, in the all-engrossing certainty of despair. Now, at last, she knew her father.

Mr. Daniel Chorley watched her awhile, then slipped quietly away to his bedchamber, and in half-an-hour afterwards was walking into the great room of the "Red Lion," up-stairs, and in the reception that there awaited him he forgot all his home annoyances.

How glad Constance was to be alone again! But no more gazing into the fire now! No more hopes—scarcely fears! The worst had come. She had been expecting it, and was prepared to meet it—at least, she thought she was —and she began to act blindly submissive to some previously formed resolve.

She sat down to write to her father, first of all, because it was the hardest thing of all to do. The tears would patter down on the paper, and the ink would run where the tears fell. She could hardly read it herself when it was finished, but it was too late to write another: so she folded it up, blotted and blistered as it was, and she stood at the street-door with it till the pot-boy came by with the next-door beer, and then gave it into his charge for her father. That done, she pinned up her skirt, and bustled about, doing all her morning's work. Then she laid his supper, and made up the fire to last some hours. After all was done that she could think of, she took her candle and went up-stairs. She spread a little shawl on the bed, and began to make up a bundle of a heap of 'Duke's clothes that were to have been sent to the school the next day, and of her own scanty wardrobe. She went and looked at her new Sunday frock, hanging behind the door, and, after some hesitation, took it down, folded and laid it in the shawl, her hands trembling as she did so; for she knew her father had bought it for her to look respectable when he took her to church, and she feared she had no right to use it for any other purpose. But she thought God would forgive her—she had so little clothes else. Then a small box, containing all her worldly treasures, must be sorted, for it was too big to put in the bundle. How tenderly she took up one little worthless trinket after another! How hard it seemed to part with any, though she knew she must! Once, as she took up something from a corner of the box, a hot mist came before her eyes, and would not let her see it; but she knew what it was that lay there in her hand so soft and silky—a tress of dark hair—her mother's hair—and again the heart struggled and resisted; but the will does not give way even to this, and the hair is put by determinedly, though very tenderly, in the Sunday frock pocket, as though it were too holy a thing to be carried about on common working-days.

And now the bundle was tied up, and she went to the bit of broken glass to put her bonnet on. The child started as she met the reflection of big, serious eyes, and looked behind her, for the face seemed more like her mother's than her own. Ah, she knew then—comprehended then—her own great change. Like seedling plants in the tropical regions, that spring up almost instantaneously to maturity, under the fierce glow of the sun and the nourishing dews or rain, she had grown in intellectual stature and force of will during the fiery and tearful ordeal she had passed through. And she knew it now—now that she was compelled to estimate herself and measure accurately all her resources. Yes, she knew she was no longer a child, but a premature woman; and she looked back in astonishment, vainly trying to recognise her former self, divided from her already by so impassable a gulf.

Well, all was done. She was ready! Ready —for what? Again the heart began to swell rebelliously, and the eyes to dart frantically from one familiar object to another in the bare dreary bedroom—the window with the one pot of some kind of seed that she was always watching for, but which never came up—the prints on the wall —the bed where her mother had so often knelt down with her and taught her to say her prayers. "Where, oh, where should she say her prayers to-night?" To silence that frightened, questioning heart that was so much trouble to her, because it was so weak and childish still, while all the rest of her had grown so old and enduring, she said to it, "Why not here?" So she knelt down. But she dared not pour out all her emotion as she had been used to do by that bed, but prayed with tightly-closed eyes, her usual evening prayer, and then raising her head, she cried aloud—

"Oh, mother! mother! is it right what I am

doing? Tell me if it isn't! Oh, mother, try and tell me!"

She stood up trembling, almost expecting, in her childish faith, some fearful sign. But none came; only the moon shone in at her window with a more calm and tender beauty than before. So, taking her bundle on her arm, she put out her candle and glided down the darkened stairs.

She touched the handle of the street-door, and then hesitated. She had forgotten to put his slippers on the fender where he liked them put. Besides, the fire must want seeing to. So she dropped her bundle on the mat, and opened the parlour-door. How bright and comfortable the place looked, with its new carpet, and pictures, and those fairy-like muslin curtains that half hid the linnet's cage! The cat, that lay curled before the fire, jumped up with her loudest purr as she entered; and the linnet, awakened by the blaze she made in stirring the fire, dropped its leg, extended its wings lazily, and sang two or three sleepy notes by way of greeting.

Everything spoke so eloquently to the trembling little heart of home—home comforts, home happiness, home peace—that it would no longer have its grief thrust back upon it, but broke out into sobs; and the weary body sank down upon the rug, and the weary head upon the stool, and the dry, aching eyes could not keep back the pressing tears any longer, so let them flow as thick and fast as they liked. Poor child! She had thought she had nothing to regret leaving— that there was nothing to regret her; and as she packed up her few things, and went about her last home duties, lo! there sprang up on every side something to claim her love, and to make the farewell more bitter to her!

But she would not long give way. She sat up on the stool and wiped her eyes; while the cat, between two dozes, glanced, with a puzzled and somewhat severe air, from her face to the comfortable fire, as if she thought the child's wretchedness inexplicable, if not wilful.

"Pussy," said the child, stroking the cat fondly the while, "I know you would let them half starve you, or cruelly beat you, before you'd run away; and so would I. But don't you remember, pussy, when the children at the big house teased your little kitten, you took it up in your teeth in the night, and brought it to me? Yes, the little one must be thought of before us, mustn't it, pussy?"

What was the child now meditating? She wiped her eyes again; and the cat declined to argue, and yawned, and stretched herself, while Constance went to the cupboard for a lump of sugar, to stick between the bars of the linnet's cage. She could not resist opening the door to stroke its feathers for the last time.

"Poor little thing! who'll feed you when I am gone?" she murmured, as it hopped upon her wrist. "But I won't leave you. We'll go together—you your way, and I mine. Go in there, and you shall be set free as soon as it is light." She put the bird gently into the empty basket which she carried on her arm, to hold what provisions she should have to buy on the long, mysterious journey she was meditating. "Good-bye, pussy! I know you're safe. You won't be starved, as dickey might be, because you're wanted for the mice.   Good-bye."

Again she looked round, but uselessly, for she was blind with tears; and then, turning away, she felt for her parcel on the door-mat, and, hanging it on her arm, she crossed the threshold of the home she was never again to enter.

Her note was put into Mr. Daniel Chorley's hands just when he was going to return thanks after the supper.   He knew the handwriting of the address, and would have been moved and agitated by the circumstance, but that he was determined nothing should interfere at that critical, that glorious moment; and so he put it into his waistcoat-pocket, and prepared himself for his speech, and delivered it, and never was he more expressive.   Everybody felt that the "old gentleman" had come out even better than they expected, notwithstanding they had expected much.   And so the note was forgotten until he got home, and had knocked at the door, and obtained no answer.   Then he wondered what Constance was about—and then he remembered

the note.   Hurriedly, by the light of the gas-
lamp, he read the blurred epistle:—

"DEAR FATHER,—Good-bye.   The key is at
Mrs. King's, next door.   Pray to God, father,
and He will bless you as He has blessed me, and
He will tell you what to do, as He has told me.
Don't write to me any more.   You can never
love me, any more.   Oh, father, I wouldn't leave
you if I wasn't sure of that !   And if you don't
love me it will make you worse now if I stay at
home, now that I know you set fire——"

The father ground his teeth, his face visibly
whitened, and an oath escaped him such as your
very respectable man alone can give utterance to
when he *is* driven to the unwonted relief.   He
looked up at and around the gas-lamp, as though
to be sure there was no living eye now reading
with him the fatal words which the child had, in
her straightforward simplicity, first written, then,
remembering how angry he would be, had tried
to blot out, but ineffectually; and so they stared
the guilty man in the face, in all their horrid
directness.   But he must read on.

" Father, I shall never come back. Don't seek me. No one shall ever hear anything about you from me. I won't even tell 'Duke. Dear father, be sure of that, and don't think any more about me. Good-bye, father.

" Your affectionate daughter,

"CONSTANCE CHORLEY."

Mr. Chorley considered a bit with himself. She had promised she would not reveal what she knew. That was well. Still better, he felt that she would keep her promise. She had especially mentioned 'Duke. The father trembled as he thought of that contingency—his boy learning of the guilty act, and showing it, possibly, by leaving him, as Constance had left. She would not tell 'Duke, she said. How could she, if she were going away at once and for ever? Ha! did she meditate—no, no, she could not, dared not! But he would visit the school in the morning, and take precautions. And as he went up to bed he began to think, while undressing himself, of what he should say, and to perceive that he should be obliged to say unpleasant things about

Constance's wilfulness and ingratitude, in expla-
nation of her disappearance; and he was vexed at
that necessity. It was too bad to have such an
almost base thing imposed upon him.   He felt
quite troubled about it, as he got into bed, and
tried vainly to compose himself. But after a
while the reverberations of the cheers in the great
room, the overflowings of the radiance and the
social glow of the evening he had just spent,
came back like a kind of Indian summer, and
enveloped his whole being; and so he went off,
at last, into a sleep, that seemed to have a voice
for him, and to whisper, " Come, come, you are
not so bad, after all. There's many a worse man
than you in the world." And he took such
assurances, as they are generally taken, to mean
—" You are a good fellow, Daniel Chorley, at
heart—on the whole, one of the best fellows
breathing." And so he slept in peace.

CHAPTER V.

WITHIN sound of the sweet minster bells, and within sight of the grey old minster towers, the old Plague-stone of Aberford lay, gathering thin yellow moss about its base, and rearing its broad bleached front high above the wayside reeds and grasses. In summer time, when the little patch of verdure beside it was fresh, and the little.clump of hawthorns all in leaf, and the merry little brook clear and full, it was a pleasant and quiet spot to come to and meditate in the grey of Sabbath evenings, when the minster bells were ringing, and a soft violet bloom lay over all the wide expanse of heath. Lovers from the town made it a trysting-place, and its white surface was one maze of rudely carven letters, mostly linked together twos and twos.

Many a bitter parting had the old stone witnessed, and sometimes in the sweet spring weather, blossoms, faint and palely luminous, sprang up so suddenly and died so soon, that one could almost fancy them a flight of loving thoughts from one of those who had gone forth along that high road to return no more; and sometimes when the wind howled over the heath by night, and drove and tugged at the immovable old Plague-stone because it would not begone before it, like the rotten leaves at its feet, you seemed to hear the wailing of a soul left standing there desolate, to watch some loved form lessening on the road, and to weep itself weary on the Plague-stone's cold rough breast.

Along this road two children were now journeying wearily.

The sun had just burst forth, and the light, fleecy clouds rolled off, leaving a sky of pale, tender blue spread out before them. The grass by the wayside was yet crisp with half-frozen dew, and the sweet air of the spring morning blew refreshingly upon the swollen eyes of the little wayfarers as they gazed upon the new world into which they were journeying hand-in-hand.

"Constance, may we rest when we get to that stone?"

"Yes, darling, and let the linnet go."

They walked on, speaking no more till they reached the Plague-stone. There they took the bird from the basket, and stroked it, and kissed it with quivering lips.

"I wonder which way it will go?" said the boy, as he stood by the stone and held the bird aloft on his fingers.

At first it only shook its feathers as if to let the fresh air penetrate them, and remained still, looking round on the green fields enjoyingly. The boy shook his hand; the bird took a little flight round and round, then perched again on the boy's finger, looked inquiringly into the children's faces, as much as to say, "Do you really want me to go?" and then broke out into delicious song.

The two looked at each other, and then at the bird, and then they burst into tears, and sat down together by the stone in silence.

"What must we do with it, Constance?" asked the boy at length, in a broken voice.

"Let it stay with us till it likes to go," answered Constance, rising and holding out her hand. "Come, 'Duke, we must push on, or we sha'n't get to the large place where I told you we must stop to-night."

They had risen and moved a couple or more paces from the stone, when they heard a hoarse voice calling behind them, and they both stood still, trembling and clinging to each other.

The girl looked round: she saw a figure approaching from the turn in the road, and her knees shook; but she said, in a firm voice—

"'Duke, it's father. Don't cry—be a man! Remember all I told you."

Another instant, and Mr. Chorley stood before them. The perspiration streamed down his face, his fine black clothes were covered with dust, and for a moment he was speechless with rage and lack of breath. Presently he gasped out—

"Constance—what—means this?"

"Father, I told you in the letter."

" But 'Duke——"

" Must go too, father."

" Why ? "

" Must I tell you before him, father ? "

" Good God ! " thought, almost said, the astounded man; " is this my daughter ? "

But he was growing too infuriated to deal with any abstract speculations now. She was evidently bent on taking away the boy he so loved and worshipped—the treasured darling for whom he had ventured so much—the very apple of his eye. Pooh! it was ridiculous ! But, unhappily, it was not the less true. There she stood, no longer shrinking. in apprehension either of him or of her own thoughts, but protecting her brother as his mother might have protected him in the presence of some dangerous animal. Yes, he saw what was in her face—what was in her eye—and he trembled inwardly, and he would have cursed her had he dared. But she was armed with a perilous, deadly weapon. What should he do? Utterly baffled, unable to speak, the miserable man presently began to weep, and lo! both the children cried too—a melancholy company.

"Come, Constance, I will treat you as a woman. You shall have your own way; I won't follow or trouble you. But leave me 'Duke; I grow old, and cannot be deprived of both my children. I can't spare him."

"You must, father."

"Why, in Heaven's name?"

"Because God says so. You will make him wicked, father! Kill me! kill me if you like, but I will say so, and God will punish you if you do! Oh, father! was it not God who gave you one chance, even at the last moment?—who prevented 'Duke from being burned by——"

"Constance!" murmured appealingly the guilty man, turning deadly pale.

"Yes, father, I understand. May we, then, go in peace?"

"Are you determined to—to——"

"I am, father!"

Mr. Daniel Chorley buried his face in his hands. He to be brought to this!—to appear thus before

his own children!—and yet to have no escape!
Suddenly, however, he said to the child—

"Come back, then, with me both, and I will
tell the whole truth, and make an end of it."

"Oh, father, will you?—will you?—will you
indeed?"

"I will."

"And forgive me afterwards? Oh, father!"
and the child was about to throw herself into his
arms, when Mr. Chorley, moved by some new
thought, or by a sense of failure as to a previous
one, said huskily, and with an affectation of
wounded pride—

"No, no, take your own way, and abide by the
consequences."

The child had not expected that, and it was the
cruellest blow of all. She sobbed convulsively
betwixt her every word as she said to the boy—

"Come then, 'Duke; kiss father, and bid him
good-bye."

And she withdrew a pace or two, as if conscious
that the father and son would have a communion
of heart in which she could not be permitted to

share. And she sat down near the old Plague-stone and waited while the miserable man held the boy in his arms, and covered him with kisses, and begged him never to forget poor papa, and received again and again the boy's heart-broken assurances that he would not. And then the father took money from his pocket—all he had there—some gold among silver and copper, and gave the whole to the boy, who threw it on the ground passionately; and then the father had to pick it all up again, and to put it into the boy's pockets, and explain that his sister would want it; and then, with one more embrace, he set the boy down, and turned to go away.

"Father!" came thrilling after him, in a tone so full of childish agony that it penetrated to his very marrow—"Father!"

He turned—hesitated—then opened his arms, and Constance, with a strange, wild cry, flung herself upon his breast, and kissed him, until he felt her arms tightening about his neck, and he got alarmed, and so he quietly unclasped them, and set her down; and she looked at him as she

stood there, motionless, upright, and rigid; and
then she looked not at him or anything else in
the world, but stared blindly on; and then she
laughed; and then there was another sad mingling and chaos of sobs and hysteric bursts from
all the three before the child grew calm.   But
she did quiet herself at last; and then Mr. Daniel
Chorley leaned back against a tree and waved
them away, unable to speak more.   Hand-in-hand
they went, and he saw their gradually lessening
forms moving further and further away from him,
until at last, when he could only just distinguish
one from the other, he saw them stop, and the
taller one take up her frock to wipe away the tears
of the shorter one, and kiss him, before they again
recommenced their march.

And now they stood upon the summit of the
distant hill; a moment more, and they would be
lost to him for ever.   He strained his eyes wildly
after them, as though they must have the power
still to keep in view those tiny specks that stood
out against the pale blue sky.   Could it be that
in another moment they would disappear for ever?

For ever ! The trees with their bursting buds, the birds swaying joyously on the branches, the little brook by the wayside dancing and gurgling with its new tide of spring showers, the heaven in the sky above looking down lovingly into the heaven in those waters below, seemed all, with one voice, to cry, with a strange joy and triumph, "For ever !"

For ever ! As the bright spring sun shone down, the earth between him and them seemed, in its glittering freshness, to smile at the parting as though it were a thing that Heaven rejoiced in, as it might rejoice for the saving of a soul. For ever!

O how the agonised heart turns and writhes, and vainly seeks to listen to the promptings of its better angel, as it whispers, "There is yet time ! Save them ! Confess all ! Bring them back !" Even in its agony it is hardened against everything but the sense of shame—discovery—acknowledgment; and so he watches, and watches, as the specks grow more and more minute, and lo ! they are gone ! On, on into life !—children, and alone ! On, on into the world !

CHAPTER VI.

THREE days had gone by since the little brook and the birds in the little clump of hawthorns had sung so merrily to the old man who sat here and wept through the sunny morning hours. Three days had gone, and in that time April had come and breathed upon the stone and wakened little pale constellations of primroses all about it.

Night was closing round the heath with great sweeps of black shadow and great gusts of angry wind. There had been service at the minster, and the little congregation seemed right glad to escape from the wild night into their homes without gossip or the customary saunter on the heath. O the delicious safety and warmth of home on such a night!

"Out in the world, children, and alone!"

Whence came that cry? There was one soli-

tary figure, silver-haired and bent, which had
made its way across the heath, and sat upon the
old Plague-stone. It was one of the little minster congregation, for a Bible and Prayer-book
lay on the ground beside him. Every moan of
the wind made him start and shiver, for it
seemed to him to be trying to utter some fearful tidings of little friendless, roofless children on
the road. To be sure he had that evening heard
the good old clergyman tell how the very
sparrows went not uncared for and unwatched,
but then, breaking in upon the comfort that
thought gave him, came a still small voice,
saying, "Into whose care gave I these little
ones?" and the grey guilty head fell into the
hands, and began listening again to the dismal
shrieking of the wind.

O the dark, wild things that that wind seemed
to hint at, as it hissed and wailed and bellowed
about his ears. Children and alone! What
might not have happened to them in those three
days?

Hark! How like a child's voice was that!

While he listened with drops starting on his forehead, the wind suddenly became like wild mocking laughter, as if to say, "How knowest thou, thou hast a child left?" and began to make a movement in the grass of the heath that suggested to him horribly the flowing back of hair from childish brows pallid and dead by the wayside.

"O God! O God!" he cried; and rose, bathed in sweat, and set his face towards the road as if no power on earth could stay him from hurrying forth to seek them, and bear with them the punishment of his crime. But lo, while he leant upon his stick trembling in every limb, he heard footsteps near him, and immediately a sense of his position returned. Hastily taking up his Bible and Prayer-book he began to move homewards, and he had not made many paces before a smile came on his face, for he seemed to know as well as if he had heard the words, that those two honest Aberford townsfolk who passed him were saying, "The grand old man, see how he comes out to meditate and worship Nature, even on such a night."

So he passed down towards the town, leaning on his stick with his right hand, and holding his Bible and Prayer-book against his heart with his left, and the lamp-lights and the merry minster bells gave him a pleasant welcome home.

And where were they who for three long days and two wild nights had travelled beyond sight of the lights of home and beyond sound of those dear minster chimes? Where were they, and what dangers beset them, that the wind wailed so dolorously round the old Plague-stone, as if calling for help and succour?

Behold where, even at this hour of the turbulent night, two little figures plash along on the road, silent, drenched, and desolate. Only three days of the world, yet what records does each pale, pinched, supernaturally aged face bear! They are silent—much too wretched to speak; but their hands clasp one another very tightly, and their little feet, as if for companionship, without effort step together. Splash—splash; it is the only sound they hear, and they listen to it till it seems to become a part of the watery

silence. It is almost like the beat of a monotonous pulse, and they have become so used to
it that their lips involuntarily count it. "One,
two—one, two;" and each "one, two" clears
about half a yard of the five miles. Weary little
feet!—when will their journey end?

Suddenly they become aware that this pulse
of the silence is not keeping the same time—that
is to say, they are counting three instead of two.
They tighten the hold of each other's hand and
look down at their feet, still counting. The left
have moved forward, "one;" now the right,
"two;" and now, before the left again moves,
there is a third splash. They dare not look back;
they go on just the same, but their hearts beat
more quickly. They feel they are not alone—
some one or something is journeying with them
along the dreary flats. Who or what is it?

The wind has ceased, yet the night is wild and
ghostly. Clouds, huge and dark, roll over the
sky in many a fantastic form. Even the tranquil
stars add to the wildness of the scene, for, as they
appear through small openings, they seem to be

the eyes belonging to those cloud-giants. The
moon is high and at its full, and is hung around
by floating hills of snow. It floods all the level,
drenched country with its white light. Here it
lights up wet, glistening heaps of broken stone,
and the black mouth of a stone quarry; here a field
in which lies the dead body of a sheep that has
died of the rot, and which, at the first peep of day,
will bring the crows screaming over the flats in
ravenous armies. Here a blighted, skeleton-like
tree is reflected vividly in a black, glassy pool by
the wayside; and there the shadow of the finger-
post projects itself right across the watery road.
Then there is the road itself lying across the
black-looking country like a curving stream. It
is visible for miles, and for miles there is nothing
upon it but three figures—two little ones on in
front, and a larger one following behind.

As is generally the case in moments of great
fear, the ears of the children have become exceedingly sharp; and they notice that the mysterious splash, which has been getting nearer
and nearer, and is now almost close up to them,

has something strange about it. Though the splash itself is heavy, they do not hear the scrunch of the boot on the loose stones; it is like the fall of a naked foot. Closer and closer it comes; they are too frightened to run— too frightened to stop; so they go on as best they may, and presently, looking down on the wet road, they see, lying there beside them, the shadow of this unknown fellow-traveller. It is that of a man, short and thick-set; and he carries a stick over his shoulder, with a pair of boots slung at the end. They stop, the shadow stops too; they begin to run, and the shadow also runs, and a gruff, drawling voice calls after them—

"Don't be afeard o' me; I'm on'y a poor man as 'ud be glad o' yer company, my young lady and gen'l'man, in these yer lonesome parts."

They hesitate and lag a little, but still keep in advance of the man, who, by his shadow, seems to limp a good deal.

"Come now, I say," he goes on in the same drawl, " you surely aint afeard on a poor man as don't want no more'n company; for now I don't see no 'arm in a young lady's and gen'l'man's stomics a-turning agin their A B C. Mine turned agin it allis, and, if so be their stomics turned agin it, why I say as it's on'y nat'ral a young lady and gen'l'man shud make off. I say as it's a plucky thing on 'em to do; and I aint the one to split on 'em, not if I knowed their schoolmissus, and their schoolmissus says to me, ' John Hollis,' she says, ' here's two made off from my school, and if you'll bring 'em back you shall be 'andsome rewarded.' No, I aint the one to split on 'em if I did know jest where they was, and 'ad seen 'em yesterday mornin' a-sitting under an 'edge a-playin' with soverings, and then had the pleasure o' spendin' a evenin' in their company at a public—not I!"

Constance turned and looked at the man, and the man looked at her, with a mocking leer on his face. She recognised him at once as a militiaman who had come upon them while they were under a tree in a retired place counting their money. Mustering up all her courage, she turned towards him, and said, faintly—

" What is it you want, please ? "

"Well, come now, I say," drawled John Hollis, keeping up with them with some difficulty, and breathing hard between each sentence; "I aint a beggar, yer know, but I'm a poor man as 'listed when he wasn't hisself for drink, and broke his poor wife's 'eart; and now, in consequence of hinjered 'ealth, 'as got 'is discharge from the army, and is now returnin' 'ome to 'is native willage, and 'is broken-'earted wife, and twelve starvin' children, without a penny in 'is pocket; and, as I said, he aint no beggar, but I make bold to say he aint above acceptin' 'elp from a young lady and gen'l'man as can play with soverings under an 'edge."

Though Constance thinks Mr. Hollis is remarkably young to be the father of so large a family, and though in the imperfect light she looks in vain to discover any signs of the "hinjured 'ealth" he speaks of in his broad fat face, she does not hesitate to draw out her purse, in the hope that a shilling will rid them of this unwelcome and loquacious companion.

"Indeed, sir," she says, "we have very little

money to take us such a long way as we've got
to go, but if that will be of any use—" And she
held it out to him timidly.

"Well, really, now," he says in his satirical
drawl, stopping their way, and holding the
shilling in his great, coarse hand, and looking
down at it with his head on one side—" well, really,
now, what a kind young lady and gen'l'man to
spare a shillin' to a poor fellow! Very 'an'some
indeed! very 'an'some. I wonder what my wife'll
say to me a-bringing 'ome such a lot o' money.
Why look here, my dears, I'll tell you what she'll
say"—and laying one hand on Constance's
shoulder and the other on 'Duke's, he leans upon
them with all his weight, and bends down till
his hot, impure breath, smelling of onions and
tobacco, defiles their faces—" yes, I'll tell you
what she'll say—when I go home my wife'll say—
I just hear her a-sayin' of it—' John,' my wife'll
say, ' what have yer got to feed yer starvin' children with?' she'll say. 'A shillin',' I'll say, ' as
was giv' me by a nice young lady and gen'l'man
a-taking a walk one night across Markham's

Medders, and as I'd seen in the mornin' a-playin' with soverings under an 'edge.' Then my wife she'll say, 'Yer fool, I'd 'a' laid hold on the young gen'l'man's arm,' she'll say "— and, to illustrate his meaning, he takes hold of 'Duke's arm in a playful manner, and fixes his eyes on Constance's pale face—" 'and I'd 'a' twisted it round and round,' she'll say." He gives 'Duke's arm a twist, and the boy utters a sharp cry, more in apprehension than real pain; but it is acute agony to Constance to hear it; and, throwing down her basket and bundle, she clutches the man's sleeve with both hands, and gazes into his brutal face with white lips and pleading eyes.

"Leave him alone! Oh, don't hurt him! You shall have more, only don't, don't hurt him!"

"'I wouldn't 'a' minded no singin' out,' my wife'll say; 'for no one wont hear ever such a singin' out across Markham's Medders; but I'd 'a' twisted it round, and round, and round till the young lady kindly forked out them soverings and every other farden she had got about her, and giv' 'em me in a purty manner,' she'll say."

Constance has fallen on her knees on the wet road, and 'Duke is still quivering in the man's grasp. One more twist of the tender arm, one more sharp cry, and soon all their little fortune lies glittering in the man's hand.

"Thank yer, my dears ; I aint a beggar, but, as I said, I aint above acceptin' 'elp when it's forced upon me by a young lady an' gen'l'man like you. Good night."

Another moment, and he is setting off across the country in a halting run, alone.

Alone ! No, no, John Hollis, not exactly alone. There is a little hand clutching at your sleeve, a faint child's voice ringing in your ears, a sweet upturned face, pale and beseeching, pictured on your guilty heart; and the hand, and the voice, and the face shall haunt you till your dying day. Never, never more, shall you be alone !

CHAPTER VII.

THE good people of Iversham boast of being the earliest risers on all the country side. Whether or no this boast be, in a general way, well grounded, it is certain that the dawn of one charming April morning found the village a very picture of life and bustle.

It was Saturday—market-day at the old town of Todness, some eight or nine miles from Iversham—and waggons, laden with the produce of those rich market-gardens, were lumbering in single file through the village, shaking its very foundations. The cracking of whips, the shouting of the waggoners, the neighing and stamping of heavy horses, the sawing and hammering in the carpenter's workshop, the nasal cries of the idiot shepherd-boy as the sheep and giddy lambs ran under the waggons, and in every direction but that in which he was trying to guide them, through the open gate of the meadow, where, standing in the bearded grass, which faintly gleamed with the earliest unexpanded buttercups, and nibbling the sweet, crisp hawthorn buds, the cows were being milked—all these noises united in making the place a perfect little Babel before Nature herself was quite awake. To all the broad valley, which lay like a garden around it, sleep seemed to cling lovingly. Even the sunbeams lay, as in a dream, aslant the wet fields and lightly-clad trees, and went stealing at a lazy pace through the pale fairy network of the woods to kiss open the eyes of all the beauteous company keeping the festivities of the season down there. A breeze of morning stirred; and the sweet hyacinth began to shake her azure bells, and the anemones and primroses all in white and star colour to lead the dance up the bank; and young ferns in palest green swayed to the music; and the hidden violet awoke with a sigh that made the breeze sink in sudden languor; and the thrush on the spray high above broke off at his sweetest note; and the happy carnival of the woods began.

There is another event, besides the fact of its being the market-day of Todness, which makes the village so early astir this morning; and this event is no less a one than the hoisting of a new sign-board at "The Waggoner's Rest." All the inhabitants, from the oldest to the baby in arms, have turned out to witness it, for it is to them a phenomenon as great as a total eclipse of the sun, or the appearance of a comet; and, indeed, they know that it would not come to pass now, had not good fortune brought hither a young man of artistic ability in the shape of the landlord's nephew.

"The Waggoner's Rest" is a little white house, with a pointed roof, surmounted by a showy gold weather-vane in the form of a greyhound, and with door and window shutters of dark green. Before it is a square of well-kept grass, fenced in by low white palings; and high above the little white gate is the iron suspender for the new sign-board. A strip of snowy stone extends across the grass from the gate to the porched door; on either side of which is a box-tree, cut and grown like a square table; and Mrs. Humphrey Standish, the landlord's wife, and the heaviest woman in the parish, boasts that each of these trees will bear her weight without "giving in." Through the low open window, left of the door, that lady's buxom form may now be seen moving about over preparations for breakfast. It is a very busy morning for Mrs. Standish; Saturday morning always is busy, for the extra hands that come over from Todness on a Friday to help pack the waggons sleep and breakfast there. Through the window, on the right of the door, they are seen sitting round a snowy table at breakfast, discussing the scraps of news they pick up from the greasy *Todness Chronicle*, which somebody brought over yesterday with sandwiches wrapped in it. The door is open, and you can see right along the red-bricked passage to the garden at the back, where pretty Madgie Standish and the young painter of the sign-board are pulling radishes under the apple-trees. Old Humphrey

Standish himself sits out on the grass-plot in front, with a slate on his knees, smoking his morning pipe, and bawls out every now and then some question to his wife, as he casts up his accounts.

In the road, a little to one side of "The Waggoner's Rest," stand two gigantic chesnut-trees, with seats round them. In the morning the children generally have the seats all to themselves to play on; in the afternoon the young girls take their needlework, and sit and gossip there; and of an evening they are left to the veterans of the village, who meet to discuss the affairs of the nation over a friendly pipe. But on this particular morning the chesnuts extend their shade over a mixed and motley assemblage, in which three generations are represented. The seats are filled for the most part by old grandmothers and grandfathers, with their hands crossed over the heads of their walking-sticks; while grouped round them stand the mothers with their children; and several boys have climbed up into the trees above for the purpose of obtaining a better view of the important proceedings about to take place at "The Waggoner's Rest."

Old Humphrey glances at them from time to time with no very kindly eye.

"What's Kit about?" he inquires of his wife through the window. "How much longer is he going to keep a mob round the place? Confound him! I wish I'd never had the thing done!"

Mrs. Standish throws down the loaf and knife she has in her hand, and soon she is seen careering down the narrow red-bricked passage like a ship in full sail; and now, completely blocking up all view of the garden as she stands in the back doorway, shading her eyes with her hand, calls loudly—

"Kit! Kit, I say! Here's your uncle wantin' to know when you're a-comin' to put up your pictur'. Don't 'ee know that all the parish is at the door to see it? Come, lad, come! As for you, Madgie, you must have left your wits in your bed this morning, to be wastin' the blessed time like this, when here's your dough all a-risin' over the top of the pan, and me got all the break-fastin' on my hands, as oughtened to have nothing to do at my time o' life. Let the radishes alone, do! and don't stand there hinderin' your cousin as is got *his* livin' to get, if you haven't yours, more's the pity. You may as well let the radishes alone, I tell you; they're too late now; Peter Bludget, as wanted 'em, has had his breakfast and gone his ways. This comes o' sending two to do a thing because one's in a hurry."

"But really, aunt," Kit is heard to protest as he approaches her, dangling a very small bunch of radishes, "we haven't been long—see, here's a bunch as big as Peter Bludget's head. I'm sure Madgie pulled most of 'em."

"Ah, Kit," says his aunt, taking them from him with a smile and a shake of the head, "you do encourage that gel in laziness and story-tellin' as if the Old Gentleman had promised you a profit on her if you get her over to him. There, go along, and take out your pictur', and I'll send Jemmy to fetch the ladder."

As Kit passed by her up the passage, Jemmy

came out of the washhouse with his hair standing on end, and his face bearing signs of a very vigorous application of the jack-towel. He was a spare little man, with one leg shorter than the other, and was deaf and dumb, yet he had served as ostler and general drudge at the "Waggoner's Rest" ever since old Standish came into the business. Jemmy was one of the most industrious, faithful, steady, punctual servants it was ever a landlord's good fortune to meet with, while he had his own way; but put him out of that, and his equal for dogged stupidity, obstinacy, and ill-temper was not to be found in any donkey that ever brayed. Old Standish himself seldom interfered with him; he saw he did his work well, and for lower wages than any one else would do it, and what more did he want from an ostler?

As a general rule, Jemmy is not accustomed to indulge in the gesticulations by which those with his infirmities are wont to express themselves. Indeed, Jemmy very rarely expresses himself at all. If his mistress forgets to give him his lunch, he never thinks of making signs for it, but stumps straightway to the pantry and helps himself; and the fear of his dirty footmarks across the kitchen keeps her memory in pretty good order concerning the matter. Moreover, it should be mentioned of Jemmy that he is never astonished at anything. The most surprising events may pass under his very eyes, yet he will take no more heed than if he had received private information at his birth of everything that is coming to pass during his lifetime.

Now, it has been one of Jemmy's ways, for no one can remember how long, to disappear into the back kitchen immediately after his breakfast; and then, after some delay, to issue from it with his face and hair in the state described, and make for the stables, in which he has a comb hidden nobody knows where. No earthly power can induce him to do aught between the two processes of washing and combing; if anything be demanded of him on his way from the washhouse to the stables, he never, by any chance, understands.

When, therefore, on this busy and important morning, Mrs. Standish, with her usual disrespect

to Jemmy's ways, lays hold of him by the breast
of his coat, and indicates to him by expressive
movements of her feet, suggestive of mounting a
ladder, what it is she wants, Jemmy, with that
peculiar facility of his of not understanding when
he doesn't choose, limps doggedly on. His mistress looks after him unutterable things as he
passes among the chickens in the stable-yard,
which lies a little to the left of the garden.

Jemmy does not enter the great stables, but
pauses before the door of a small compartment
under the hay-loft. This is no longer used as a
stable, on account of the wall at the back having
given way and exposed it to the road; so it is now
made a receptacle for empty sacks and old horse-
cloths, and smells agreeably of hay and old bass.
Jemmy opens the door, takes one step forward,
then limps back about two yards with a rapidity
that astonishes his mistress.

" What's the matter with the old fool now ? "
she says to Madgie, who is looking up the passage
after Kit.

Jemmy stood where he was for more than a

minute, scratching his head and staring before him into the sack room; then he turned and limped up the yard at a rate which struck wonder into all the chickens, and caused them to use their wings as well as their legs in getting out of his way. Stopping close to Mrs. Standish and Madgie, he jerked his thumb over his shoulder in the direction of the sack room some seven or eight times in a most mysterious and emphatic manner.

" Oh, goodness gracious, mother ! What's the matter with him ? " cried Madgie, turning pale.

" Go and fetch your father and cousin directly," said Mrs. Standish; and grasping Jemmy by the arm, she went sailing down the yard with him. Madgie soon came running back with her father and Kit, and she and her mother let the men go on in advance and take the first look.

" What is it, father? Oh! what is it ? " said Madgie, going behind him.

Old Standish let his pipe fall and smash to atoms as he peeped in at the door.

" Why, here's a couple of children dead on the bass ! " he exclaimed.

A low, buzzing murmur of horror ran through the group, and they all came crowding round the door.

"God help us, father! what's come on us now?" said Mrs. Standish, catching hold of her husband's arm with both hands, and trembling all over. "Are you sure they're dead?"

"Let's get 'em to the kitchen fire, mother," said Madgie, her pretty face more subdued than Kit had ever seen it before. "Make haste—let's get them into the warm—perhaps they are only asleep or fainted."

At this moment, Jemmy, who, instead of standing looking with the others, had been and fetched the wheelbarrow from round the corner, came up with it, and began to elbow his way between his master and mistress into the sack room, Madgie following him.

This move aroused old Standish from his temporary fit of abstraction. Seizing Jemmy by the collar of his coat, he dragged him back out of the shed, and, barring his daughter's progress by half shutting the door, planted his back against it, and addressed them in the following manner:—

"Wait a bit—wait a bit—hold off all of you, and hear what I've got to say. Look you here— there's two sides to the question about touching them at all. They may be dead, or they may not, but appeariantly they are dead. I'd be loth to leave 'em if they wasn't; but there's such a thing as a correnor's inquest; and I've met more than one in my life who has found it turn out awk'ard for them touching dead bodies. Now, how do I know it mayn't turn out awk'ard for me, being found on my premises and all? No, no; I mean to be on the safe side. Leave 'em alone, and I'll go up to Todness for Justice Huffer, and here's Kit to stand witness to our not having laid a finger on 'em."

"I'll be hanged if there is, though!" cried Kit. "A pretty figure for a fellow to cut in a court of justice, standing witness to leaving two children in a place like this without knowing if they're dead or alive! Let's come by!"

Jerking open the crazy door with a force that nearly upset his uncle's balance, Kit stepped lightly over the sacks and rubbish, and kneeled down beside the two still and childish forms lying on the bass.

The sunshine gushing in at the wide-open door, and meeting that which found its way through the break in the wall, filled the little place with a sudden glare of light, revealing the husks of barley on the floor, and sending the spiders that were swinging leisurely in mid-air, rushing up invisible ladders, to take refuge in their black waving hammocks suspended from the roof. The only things in the sack room as yet undisturbed by the light were the children. The shadows of the long grass growing between the road and the shed waved fitfully over the light-coloured matting on which they lay; and as a background to the strange picture, there appeared, through the break in the wall, a glimpse of the valley, with its silvery, winding river, and vivid spring foliage and pastures, all swimming over with April sunshine.

But Kit did not look towards this, for his whole attention was taken up by the strange travellers. He looked first at the long, straight figure of the one, with the black frock falling scantily about it, and the pale, careworn, but unconscious little face, with the short black hair lying in rings upon the forehead; and then at the fair small head of the other traveller, whose hair was being lifted and played with by the sunshine and breeze together, till it seemed like a maze of golden threads.

He looked at them both, and at their travel-soiled clothes, and a series of curious expressions flitted over his face. He did not say anything, but took hold of the little one's arm, and shook it gently. The child opened a pair of heavy blue eyes, and fixed them wonderingly on the young man's face.

"Christopher," he said, "is it you? I thought it was him twisting my arm round."

"Who, my little man?" inquired the landlord's nephew, kindly.

The boy did not answer, for he was looking at his sister, who lay as calm and unconscious of the glaring daylight and the voices as a graven image. Then, too, he saw the strange faces clustered round the door, and he murmured, with a cold fear creeping over him, and trembling the while from head to foot—

"What are they looking at, Christopher? Is she—is Conny——?"

His wild blue eyes supplied that last word of the question which his lips refused to utter. Christopher did not attempt to make any answer, but, sliding a not very steady arm under the girl, raised her up gently. His arm shook still more, and a murmur escaped Mrs. Standish and Madgie, as they saw her head droop back and her arms hanging stiffly down.

"Make way," said Kit, hastily. "It's old Chorley the bookseller's daughter, at Aberford; the very girl I took out o' the fire!" Then raising her in his arms like a babe, he carried her out into the air. 'Duke kept close to him, and the rest followed him up the stable-yard and into the kitchen.

When, on the night before, Constance had taken refuge, with her brother, in the strange resting-place where Jemmy found them, all fortitude, all hope, had left her heart. She let 'Duke cry himself to sleep without uttering one word of comfort, and, covering him with her shawl, turned away, and sat with her hands clasped in her lap, looking out of the broken wall at the two or three solitary lights _twinkling far away down in the valley. She could not sleep, she could not pray, for one spectre was before her eyes that held them open, and one word alone came to her lips, and they repeated it over and over, each time with keener shame and misery—" Beggars! beggars!" That was all she felt; they were beggars; and if little 'Duke had found the journey hard before, what would it be for him now? How would she find a resting-place for him at night? —how keep him from that terrible spectre which fear and hunger already brought near to her— _starvation?_ And now, for the first time, her heart yearned, for his sake, towards the old home, and became heavy with doubt as to whether she had done well in taking him from its shelter. Suppose he should die of the journey, as the poor little linnet had! How would life be endurable

to her ever after? She lifted her streaming face
and clasped hands heavenwards, as if trying to
reach again that invisible guiding Hand, which
seemed to have let go of her when she most
needed its aid. It was two hours before she fell
asleep, for the sack room was not so quiet a
resting-place as might be imagined. The water
dripping incessantly from the roof, the horses
stamping in the adjoining stable, the yard-dog
jangling his heavy chain, and the rats galloping
on the granary-floor overhead, kept her awake
till the reflection of the stars faded in the river,
a new light began to kindle it, and the dark
valley shaped itself into fields and meadows. Then
she slept, and dreamed she was again in her own
little bed behind the picture-screen in the attic at
home.

Her eyes had been closed scarcely an hour
when she was awakened by the loud cackling of
the hens in the stable-yard. Faint with hunger
and weariness, she raised herself on her elbow,
and gazed around her in bewilderment, perfectly
unconscious of where she was. Then, when her

eyes fell upon Jemmy's extraordinary face in the doorway, a remembrance of all that had befallen her flashed across her mind, and, uttering a low moan, she fell back senseless on the matting.

When consciousness again returned, it seemed to the child that she was in another world. The first thing she became aware of, on opening her eyes, was a glare of yellow crocuses. She was lying on the great linen-press, under the open window of the kitchen; and it seemed to be the fresh breeze blowing on her face that was bringing her slowly and tranquilly back to life. She heard many voices laughing and talking without, and Constance, impelled by a childish curiosity, endeavoured to raise herself up to a sitting posture, that she might see what was going on. She did so with difficulty, and, leaning her head at the side of the window, looked over the yellow crocuses.

There was upon her that dreamy half-consciousness in which we can see or hear all things with mute acquiescence. She looked out upon the busy village picture, surrounded by country more beautiful than she had ever seen in the whole course of her dreary little life, and a vague wonder and delight lit up her dark eyes. Was it a dream? 'Duke laughing and happy there amongst the children; these beautiful flowers, which seemed to shine upon her and comfort her like the sun; the fair spreading valley, of which she only caught delicious glimpses under and between the great waggons; the vivid blue of the April sky— yes, a dream surely it all must be. But presently, as she gazed up at the dazzling white clouds flitting like angels' robes over the blue, there appeared between her eyes and that sky a face the sight of which made the child's heart leap within her. Her eyes kindled, not with the slow recognition of a once-familiar face almost for- gotten, but with the wonder and joy of meeting suddenly, in the flesh and the life, a face which, in the space of a moment, when she lay as in the valley of the shadow of death, when those flames leapt around her, and that fiery sword hung over her, had been photographed on her heart for ever. And long she sat there gazing up at him with that look which made Christopher smile, and praying that, if all were, indeed, a dream, she might never awake to find it so.

Alas, poor little Poplar! Even while she gazed, the sky darkened over with a fit of April passion, great rain-drops fell thick and fast, the waggoners ceased to admire the newly-mounted sign, cracked their whips, and the waggons lumbered on, leaving the valley, with its lustre all dimmed, open to the view. Women threw their skirts over their heads, and rushed to their several homes with the young children; the boys dropped out of the branches, shaking down showers of bursting buds; the carpenter went on sawing his plank; Jemmy hobbled to the stables with a sack over his shoulders; and Humphrey Standish, with his wife, and Madgie, and Christopher holding 'Duke by the hand, entered the kitchen of the "Waggoner's Rest."

"Sit down, lass—sit down," said Mrs. Standish, laying her hand on her shoulder, and gently forcing her back on the edge of the press.

"You don't look as if your legs 'ud bear you yet."

It was the first kind word, the first kind touch, the poor child had known for many a long day, and it brought the image of her mother floating before her eyes. She sat still a minute or more, looking down, and plaiting and unplaiting her thin, brown fingers, then, turning her face over her shoulder, burst into tears. 'Duke turned round and gazed at her in amazement; Christopher looked troubled, and the three judges by the linen-press exchanged meaning glances. To them it was evident her tears were a silent confession of some wrong-doing having brought her and her little brother into this strange position.

"Come now, missy, don't cry," said Mrs. Standish, trying to speak severely, in order to prevent her husband doing so—"don't cry, but speak out and tell us how you come to be strayin' away from your home like this. Don't you think it's a very dreadful thing? and your poor little brother so delicate too, bless him! Come, tell us all about it— where you come from, and where you *was* going."

But while Constance stood silent, wondering what she could say, Kit seemed to be urging something on Humphrey, apart, in an undertone too low for Constance to catch a word.

At last the innkeeper rose, and laying his pipe on the mantelpiece, and putting his foot on his chair to tie his shoe, said, with his back towards them—

"Well, I don't know as I mind that—I don't know as I mind doing as Kit says—let 'em be here then till to-morrow, when Kit's father and mother's coming to dinner, and then we'll talk over what's to come of 'em. As Kit says he's seen 'em with respectable people, I don't know as I mind 'em stayin' till then—no, I don't know as I do."

Constance was about to thank him, but he had passed out of the room before she had thought of a word to say.

CHAPTER VIII.

IT was drawing nigh to the early tea-hour at
"The Waggoner's Rest." Constance sat alone
in the kitchen, at the little side-table containing
Madgie's Bible and workbox, with a heap of
stockings before her. All the noise and bustle
of the market-day was over. Humphrey Standish
and his wife dozed by the fire in the best
parlour, undisturbed by Jemmy's splashing and
scrubbing in the stable-yard, or the clink clink
of the little maid's pattens on the bricks of the
passage and washhouse. Madgie, with 'Duke by
her side, sat at needlework under the chestnuts,
and Christopher was leaning over the white
palings, chatting and laughing with her and her
companion. Now and then those busy brown
fingers in the kitchen would pause over their

work, and those large, earnest eyes be lifted from
the stocking and allowed to rest one moment on
his face; often they would be turned to their
work again full of tears, for the child's heart
was very sorrowful when she felt that Christopher
would never know that the life he had saved was
being devoted to a good purpose, but must always
think she had run away with some secret disgrace
upon her, as was now probably being hinted in
Aberford. Yes, she was very sorrowful when she
thought of this, and turned over in her mind all
manner of things to say to him; but she could
perceive no way to convince him save by revealing
her secret, and, rather than do that, she would
endure the scorn of Christopher and all the world.
So she tried to forget it for a time, and bent
resolutely over old Humphrey's grey stocking.
But the sound of the girls' happy voices, laughing
and chattering in the sunshine, made her thoughts
wander, and presently she looked up again.
Christopher had left the gate, and she heard his
step coming up the passage. Her hand shook
so that she could scarcely guide her needle, for

she felt that if he found her alone, he would question her about the object of her journey, and how should she answer him?

In another minute she heard him crossing the kitchen with his shaggy dog, Merrylegs. 'Duke followed with a ship which Kit had rudely fashioned for him, and wanted to know when he would take him down to the river to sail it.

"Oh, we'll see about that after tea," Christopher said, smiling at the air of intense relief which Constance could not conceal at the interruption.

" And, Conny, you must come too," said 'Duke, patronisingly. "May my sister come with us, Christopher ? "

" Certainly."

" And Merrylegs? "

" Well, yes, Merrylegs can come, if your sister has no objection." This was said a little mischievously, for the Poplar and Merrylegs had been by no means good friends at Aberford, where he flew at her heels almost every time she went out.

"I'll answer for his being on his best behaviour.
I'm going up to Hollington now, but will meet
you at the water-side when you've done your teas.
Good-bye for the present."

"Good-bye, Christopher," said the child; "we
will be sure to be there"—and her face flushed
and lighted up with a ray of genuine pleasure
as she once more bent over her work—and oh,
how the little brown fingers flew! A vision
floated before her eyes—a vision of the shining
river, with its pale green banks, where she was
going to walk with Christopher, in the still
evening, and taste her first and last of liberty,
and rest, and peace, before work, real hard work,
must begin. Yes, the fingers flew, and so fast,
and so deftly, that, when Madgie came in with
the milk for tea, the grey stockings were finished,
and the little seamstress was ready to assist in
preparing that comfortable meal.

"Where's Kit?" inquired the landlord, as he
sat down at the table and saw his nephew's place
empty.

"Oh, gone to look at Mister Dale's new

threshing-machine; there's something wrong with it, and they've sent for him," answered his wife.

"I wish folks 'ud leave him to keep to his own trade, and not go making him think he can understand everything. What does he know about engineerin'?"

Constance thought tea would never be over. She saw, through the back window, the shadows creeping higher and higher up the stable wall, and, at the front, she saw the crocuses closing, and feared that all the brightness and sparkle must die out of the valley before they reached the river-side.

"Where are *you* going, young sir?" inquired the landlord, as 'Duke, when the meal was over, got down from his chair, and took his ship in his arms.

"He is going to try his ship in the river, please," Constance answered for him, quite at a loss how to ask leave for herself.

"Then get on your bonnet, lass, and go with him," said Mrs. Standish, kindly. "It's pleasant down there by the water-side; go—it'll do you good."

So they went out together joyfully, and up the quiet village street, passing the chestnuts, where the old men sat, and the prim church, and the school, and then over the stile, and through the hushed market-gardens and fields that went slanting down to the river. They came upon it suddenly at last, for, as they had got low in the valley, the thickening trees had hidden it from their view; but now, through a break in the foliage, they came upon it, and stood on its brink, following with thoughtful eyes the shining little waves as they rolled along.

Just here the river seemed to have a separate world of its own, shut in from the outer world by ranks of trees towering grandly one above another, till the chestnuts showed their pale, crimped leaves against the sky. Though, as Constance had feared, the sunshine had died away from the spring foliage and the water, she did not miss it, for this river-world possessed a faint, mysterious lustre of its own. It seemed to Constance that every tree—from the limes and chestnuts high above, to the willows and young aspens fringing the banks—gave forth a light of its own, each tender and faint, but each different. The white buds on the blackthorn glimmered like strings of pearls, and the tufts of primroses shone clear and luminous on the river's brink, like a reflection of the coming stars; the water itself kept breaking into little circles of silver light, as the trout leaped in it, snatching at the gnats buzzing and whirling above. And even as the light of day, so also the sounds of day, were not missed, for the river sang as it flowed—sang in its strong, calm voice, reminding one of a happy life flowing on and on, in faith and strength, to the sea of eternity. And Constance sat down on the stone beside it, and listened to it, and drew comfort and peace from its song.

She had not sat there many minutes, listening to the river, and watching 'Duke flitting hither and thither along the bank, before her ear caught another sound, and she smiled without taking her eyes from the grey water. It was Christopher's whistle—that same clear, brilliant whistle she had often and often listened to as she sat at her little bedroom window in the early summer mornings at Aberford. She smiled to herself now as she remembered how she used to wonder who it was that whistled with such wonderful clearness and accuracy, and how she mingled this whistle with the wild old romances she used to take, one by one, from her father's shop, and read and dream over in her dreary attic.

"Hullo!" shouted Christopher, leaping down the bank, with Merrylegs after him. "What, here first?"

She looked up, and made room for him on the stone; and, being tired, Christopher sat down, and Merrylegs went tearing off to where he saw 'Duke, far away along the bank, looking like a speck on the water's edge. Christopher took up the ship from where it rested against Constance's feet, and, while examining it and tightening the sails, broke out again with a whistle, not sharp nor brilliant now, but modulated to the low, soft, river music, and the sighing of the trees as the wind made their crisp young leaves brush together. Truly there must be music in Christopher's soul, Constance thought (though she could not put her thoughts into words), as she gazed up in his face with childish wonder and awe, that he was thus able to make his whistle blend so perfectly with the trees and the river, that it no more destroyed the harmony than did the waving of the rushes, or the breathing of the blue hyacinths.

"Christopher," she said, under her breath, and without moving her wondering eyes from his face,—"Christopher, I wish you would sing the same thing that you are whistling. Are there words to it?"

Christopher looked at her in surprise.

"What was I whistling?" he asked.

"I don't know. It was a soft, sad tune, like the sound of the water."

"Was it this?"

And, setting down the ship, and leaning his head on his hand, he hummed the refrain of a plaintive old love-song that Constance had often heard her mother sing over her work long years ago, and she looked up in tears, and nodded for him to go on, though it was not the air he had been whistling; and then Christopher, smiling at her earnestness, began the first line of the song, and sang it through, in a voice so full, and sweet, and exquisitely modulated, that the "Little Poplar" was too much stirred to sit still. She rose up on the stone, and stood listening, with her brown hands clasped, and eyes brimming over with tears, while the sound flowed round her; and it did not seem to be Christopher alone who sang, but the river and the reeds along its brink. The sighing willows and rustling hawthorns, taking their key-note from his voice, seemed to swell the sound till it filled all the little river-world, and rose up—up—beyond the limes— beyond the highest chestnuts, and out into the blue space where the evening star shone all alone in its tender beauty. Yes, the "Little Poplar" wept, for her heart struggled and rebelled under its heavy weight of care, and yearned with a strong and passionate yearning to be released.

" Why did you tell me life was all dark and bitter ? " it cried to her. " Is there such beauty and joy in it as this I feel go by me, and must I be shut out from it for ever and ever ? " At that instant, as she stood there, she might, indeed, have been the poplar, and Christopher's voice might have been the south wind whispering round it, laden with the sweet odour of distant hay-fields and bruised clover, and making it moan and lash the sky, and turn this way and that, in wild longing, as it hears of all the wondrous wealth of summer beauty lying beyond its desolate wold.

Christopher finished his song; the last notes died away down the river, and lingered quiveringly among the rushes, as on the strings of a harp; yet the dark, lithe figure on the stone stood motionless. He had watched it all the while he sang, and thought how eerie and elf-like it looked, as the wind blew its scant robe and short, jetty hair all one way, showing the sharp outline of its face and form. As he looked at her now, without knowing whether he had pleased or pained, she met his eye, and, crouching down upon the stone, hid her face in her hands, and he could hear her low, half-stifled sobbing. ·Christopher was much perplexed; never having had a sister of his own, he understood nothing of the nature of little girls, and generally disliked and avoided them, Madgie alone excepted; but then she was two years older than himself, and of a calm, lazy temper that never troubled any one. Yet, though they annoyed and perplexed him, these outbursts of the " Little Poplar " seemed to tell of an earnest, passionate nature that was not without its charm to him, strange and new as it was.   He looked at the young form that, on the night of the fire, he had borne in his arms as a dead thing—looked at it bowed down beside him. A wish, too strong to spring merely from curiosity, possessed him to fathom the mystery that enshrouded it.   He hardly knew the sound of his own voice as he touched her on the shoulder, and said—

"What is the matter? Why don't you tell me?"

Constance did not move, but the strange, sweet kindness of Christopher's voice went straight to her heart, and a great lull came over her—such a lull as fell upon the troubled waters when One said unto them, " Peace, be still." Would she hear that voice again—just the same, low and somewhat unsteady, but oh, so sweet, so very sweet, for its kindness? She sat still, waiting, in trembling, happy silence.

" Come, let me help you, if I can. You could trust me, couldn't you?"

She raised her face, just as it was, wet with tears, and radiant in its happiness, and looked into his.

" Christopher!" she said, " do you remember that dreadful, dreadful night?"

" Look!" said Christopher, smiling, and holding out his hand.

She bent over it, and he saw her lips turn white and quiver as she looked at the half-healed burn.

" For me," she murmured—"for me. Oh, Christopher!"

"Well," said Christopher, laughing, "I don't suppose it would have pained the less, if it had been for anybody else. But what about that night, then?"

"You asked me, Christopher, if I could trust you, and I was going to tell you that, since that night, I have felt as if I could trust you before any one in the world, because you were the only one in the world who thought me worth risking life for."

"Well, then," returned Christopher, "if you really feel so, Pop—Constance, I mean—tell me what all this is about."

"All I can tell you, Christopher," she answered with mournful firmness, "is this: I have him"—and she pointed to 'Duke, who was guiding his ship, which he had taken away while Christopher was singing, along the edge of the river—"I have him to work for and bring up all by myself. We have no home, no father—yes, yes, I know what you mean—he lives, but I tell you we haven't any father—no, Christopher, we are alone in the world."

"Then, of course," said Christopher, "if that's all I'm to know, it's impossible for me to help you, with my uncle."

Those large, liquid eyes, gazing down at the river, grew so full of anguish and despair, that he half repented of the tone in which this was said.

"Ah, Christopher, Christopher, how I wish, oh, how I wish, there'd never been a lie told since the world began—so that you wouldn't think, so that you wouldn't dream, of disbelieving me when I tell you that, as sure as there is a river at our feet, as sure as there is a God in heaven, Christopher, it is not anything I have done that has brought us to this. If it were, Christopher, and if it were for myself that I have left home and him, I couldn't have borne all that I have—I must have gone back long before. I couldn't feel this great thankfulness to you, Christopher, for saving me that night, but should hate you for not having left me to die."

It was not easy to sit there and listen to that childish voice, and doubt the truth of what it uttered with such passionate vehemence; nor to look into that childish face without perceiving that it was conscious truth ennobled it.

"Constance Chorley," said Christopher, forgetting for the moment she was a child, "I do believe you. I promise I will help you in whatever I can, without wanting to know more."

"You do?—you will?" she said, and such a smile illumined the sallow little face! He had seen that smile twice before—once when she lay under the fiery beam, and once when she looked at him from the window of "The Waggoner's Rest." He had thought then it must have been the glare of the yellow crocuses that gave it its strange charm; but now he could see it was the heart's own sunshine breaking through the clouds.

"Then you are satisfied now?" he said, smiling also. He half expected another outburst of gratitude, but she merely nodded as she looked down the river, and answered, in a low, quivering tone—

"Yes, Christopher, thank you—quite—quite satisfied."

'Duke shouted and sang to his little fairy ship. The daylight fled, and the pale moonbeams stole in through the branches, and each leaf and flower gave forth a lustre more soft and bright than ever.

It was strangely out of keeping with Christopher's restless nature to spend two whole hours in idleness, and he could not understand how they had passed so quickly, nor could he understand the dreamy, exquisite pleasure which stole over him with the voice of the river and the faint moonlight. Was it thoughts of Madgie? Perhaps it was. Constance wondered—he wondered himself—if he had been fancying that quiet little companion at his side, across whose clear brow and cheek flickered shadows of the overhanging leaves, to be his cousin Madgie. He was half inclined to believe he had.

And yet, when in his dreams that night, and long after, the sweet April evening and the shining river came before him, it was not that cabbage-rose face of Madgie's, with its lips reminding one of the cherry season, and roving blue eyes, but a little face as pure and fragile as the hawthorn-blossom that he looked for in his vision—a little face with a thin, pensive mouth, and dark eyes swimming in happy, holy light.

CHAPTER IX.

A FAMILY CONSULTATION DINNER.

EVER since the Vallons and the Standishes had been allied by marriage, the custom was, when any important family business had to be settled, to hold a consultation-dinner at "The Waggoner's Rest." Kit remembered several of these dinners —indeed, more than one had been holden on his account; but not a single instance could he recollect when he had not felt considerably greater interest in pondering and conjecturing what lay beneath the bright, but battered, old dish-covers, than in listening to the discussion carried on by his elders. Now however, when, on this first Sunday in the eighteenth April of his existence, his relatives were gathered together to decide by which of the numerous handicrafts he practised he should earn his bread through life, he felt, as he sat before his untouched dinner, that peculiar strain at his waistcoat-buttons which in former times he never knew until after the third course of pudding. In vain he tried, by chatting lightly with Madgie, to keep up an appearance of unconcern; his hands shook as he passed the loaded plates to their various destinations, and all he said wanted point. His aunt and uncle saw and attributed his unusual behaviour to simple excitement, but his mother's soft brown eyes were fixed upon his face with a look that showed sympathy with a much deeper feeling she knew to be astir in Kit's heart just now. Up to this day Kit's life had been one bright advance. *He* knew no regretful yearnings after the past. If he looked back at all, it was to view with pleasure the progress he had made, for nothing did it contain brighter than what he saw in the future. If yesterday took a hope away, to-day brought a more radiant one to lead him on. But he knew that a time had come when this bright advance must stop —when his airy dreams must be confined within the narrow limits of the workshop—when the line of social distinction, which his eyes as yet had scorned to see, should be made for ever impassable —and, as he looked into the gleaming cover where passed before his eyes a series of consultation-dinners, marking all the important stages of the " set grey life " he was about to enter upon, far in the future he saw himself sitting at the end of the table—where his father sat—deciding the fate of *his* son. And would it go on so for ever ? he asked himself. Were his sons, for generation after generation, to sit at that table and make their choice, simply between the mallet and the spade, the shop and the plough ? Yes, Kit asked himself these questions, and a spirit of rebellion, against he knew not what, swelled his heart.

During these consultation-dinners it was customary to allow the company to take off the edge of their appetites before commencing business. Then, ere the second tending of meat, Grandfather Vallon arose and drew attention, by an appropriate speech, to the occasion which had brought them together.

All manner of noises filled Kit's ears, and a film came across his eyes as he saw the tall, lanky figure of his grandfather rise and stick its yellow fists on the table, and bend over it; and, one by one, each knife and fork ceased to clatter, and was laid in brief repose across the plate. Humphrey Standish covered over the great round of beef that was before him, and leaned forward with his arms on the table. Mrs. Standish laid a finger on her cheek, and assumed an air of grave responsibility. Mrs. Vallon, Kit's mother, had enough to do to keep the baby from crawling right across the table to its grandfather, who, it fancied, invited its approach.

"Humphrey Standish," began old Vallon, looking, not at the landlord, but at his son Jack, who now and then encouraged him in his speech with nods and—"Right, right—just so, just so"— "Humphrey Standish, according to the old, original rule——"

"Yes, yes—just so," said Uncle Vallon, with an approving nod.

"My family," proceeded old Vallon, "is come over for the purpose of consulting your family on an event, or a piece of business——"

There he paused, and looked doubtfully at Jack.

"Yes, yes—it doesn't matter which; go on—event, or piece of business."

"Likely to prove of great importance to both families."

"Ay, that's very true," said Mrs. Standish, emphatically, wiping her eyes as she looked at Madgie and Christopher. "Go on, grandfather."

"And this event is," old Vallon proceeded, "the deciding on some respectable trade for my dear grandson, Christopher, by which he may earn his bread like an honest man, as his father, and grandfather, and great-grandfather did before him. There, Jack! I think that's what you wanted me to put before Humphrey Standish, isn't it?"

And grandfather sat down and wiped his forehead.

"Yes," said Uncle Vallon; "I think grandfather's put it all before you very neat; and now, Standish and Margaret, what say you?"

"I say this," answered Mrs. Standish, folding her arms, and gazing admiringly at Kit, "that there never was, nor never will be, a lad so hard to choose a trade for as him; and why? because he's got every trade going at his fingers' ends. I'm sure, where he picked 'em all up beats me to this day. One time I see him mendin' Madgie's little table, and I says to Humphrey, ' Oh, there's no doubt about it, Kit's heart and soul a joiner!' but turn my back a minute, and there's the old clock on the stairs, as stopped a week before he was born, a-tickin' as if there had been nothing the matter with it! But Lor'! it's the same with everything; and, as I say, how did he come by it all? How came he to understand everything like this, from the Latin gibberish in his prize grammar to the workings of a clock's inside? He goes about things in such a knowing, easy way, and looks at 'em as much as to say, ' I understand all about you—don't have any nonsense with me!'—and, if you'll believe me, I can't help fancying, sometimes, when I'm expecting of him down, that the clocks keep better time, and the doors stop creaking, as if they was afraid of him."

" Ay, ay—that's all very well," said the land-lord; " but he won't get a honest living by being a Jack-of-all-trades—that's quite certain."

" Well, and what's your advice, Humphrey ? " asked Uncle Vallon.

" Why, that he sticks to his father's busi-ness, and knocks all the other nonsense out of him."

All the company looked at Kit and Kit's father, to see what they thought of this advice. The son remained immovable, with his eyes dull and fixed —not a shadow of a smile had his aunt's rhapsody brought forth on his face. The father leaned his elbow on the table, and his bright black eyes searchingly and seriously gazed into the uncertain grey ones of the landlord.

" How do you mean, Humphrey Standish ? " said he, in a tone of mild reproof. " Why do you call the talents it has pleased God to give my boy nonsense ? "

" Because they seem as if they'd keep him from

settling to one honest trade," growled the land-lord.

"Stay! I think, Humphrey, you are wrong there," said Uncle Vallon, a little excitedly.

"Perhaps you have made up your mind," said the landlord, shortly; "because, if you have, you had better tell us at once, and not go asking advice just to puff it away."

"Yes, Humphrey Standish," Kit's father answered, quietly but firmly—"I have made up my mind."

Jack Vallon made up his mind on such an important affair as this, and before a consultation-dinner had been held upon it! His father, sister, and brother-in-law—nay, even his own wife and Kit—were overwhelmed with amazement, and fell to wondering whatever would come next.

"And pray what might your mind be?" inquired the landlord, as soon as his astonishment found voice; and every eye, save Kit's, was turned upon Uncle Vallon.

The wheelwright hemmed and coughed as if he had got something in his throat he couldn't swallow; and the upper halves of his cheeks, which were not concealed in his stiff stand-up collar, became, by turns, red and pale. Kit, in the midst of his anxiety, was aware that Madgie was laughing in her sleeve at his father's ridiculous appearance just now, with his hands twitching one another, and the long daffodil all a-tremble in his button-hole. It was the last time in his life Kit was ashamed of his father. Suddenly, as they all looked at him, as at one whose brain had given way, Uncle Vallon threw off his nervous, hesitating manner, and, leaning forward, with his hands clasped on the table, and turning his eyes, brimful of modest pride and tenderness, upon his son, said, in a voice loud and distinct, but trembling with emotion—

"Yes, I have decided on what I will make of Christopher: not a carpenter, though I humbly believe he wouldn't find his equal, if I did; nor yet a wheelwright, though he could shame his father. He knows much; but, to be that which I would make him, he must know much more—must labour and strive harder than he has ever

done yet.   It's no trade I am going to put him to
—it's a profession."

"A profession!" was echoed on all sides.

"Yes, I am going to put him in a position to
fight his way amongst the best of 'em.   I've got
the money to do it—money earned by the sweat
of my brow on purpose for him, when I might
have been taking my rest—and I will do it!   Yes,
Humphrey Standish, with God's blessing, I will
make my son an engineer and a gentleman!"

Christopher sat still, looking down into his
plate, all unconscious of the amazement, the
panic, which followed his father's speech; his
very soul seemed to reel with the giddiness of
a bird burst from its long imprisonment into
boundless space.

The landlord rose to his feet, trembling with
some unaccountable emotion :—

"Jack Vallon, you're a fool!" he said, hoarsely.

His brother-in-law regarded him in pained,
stern surprise.

"Humphrey, what is the matter with you?"

"Matter, Jack Vallon!   I take it to heart, this

yer. I thought better on you, Jack—I thought better things on you. Make him a gentleman ! Are you so fond o' the tribe as you'd make more on 'em to suck the poor? Is that your speret, Jack?—is that your grandfather's speret?"

"Listen, Humphrey!" said Jack. "I have my reasons for doing this thing."

"I don't want to hear 'em!" cried the landlord, almost passionately. "I put this to you, what'll the people as he's to go among say to his family? Ah, I put that to you:—'What's your father?' 'A wheelwright.' 'And what was your grandfather?' 'A carpenter.' 'And your great-grandfather?' 'A tramping tinker.' Fine ancestors for a gentleman, eh, Kit? Tush! Jack, I tell you they'll none of him; he'll be trod under their feet like dirt. I thought you'd 'a had more pride for your family."

"I am sorry to say it, Humphrey Standish," Jack returned, shaking his head mournfully; "but, to tell the truth, leaving out o' the question what Kit may do, I haven't much cause to be proud o' my family. They've mostly been of that set o' men who have 'My son sha'n't be better than me' for their motto, and act upon it age after age—a set that wouldn't thank you for bettering of them. No, Humphrey, I've no call to be proud of my ancestors, but my grandsons sha'n't say that. We'll get out o' this somehow, or, if not, they shall know that Jack Vallon, the wheelwright, made a hard push for it."

"And pray," said Humphrey, with a scarcely-concealed sneer, "how is this fine scheme to be managed?"

"Why, Gwynne and Hardell, the great agricultural machine-makers, have seen Kit two or three times, and taken a fancy to him, and I have agreed to pay them a pretty stiff premium."

"Ay, indeed; and how much, now?"

"Why," said Uncle Vallon, after a moment's hesitation, as if to pluck up courage, "I know I have done well; for I am to pay only half of what their last pupil paid them." Still he did not mention the sum, but wiped his warm face, and seemed to forget the question had been put.

"But the figure, Jack?" remorselessly continued Humphrey.

"Well, it's a stiffish sum, as I said. No less than £200—but there are many advantages."

Humphrey gave a prolonged whistle, and Mrs. Standish coughed rather gravely, and altogether there was an uncomfortable idea pervading the place that Uncle Vallon had done a wild thing. But the latter sat quiet, and ceased speaking.

With his hands clasped between his knees, looking down upon the floor, Christopher all this while had never once raised his eyes. Whether he was abashed by his father's confidence, or whether he felt an unworkmanlike sensation of something pressing at his lids, I cannot say, but now he raised them, and turned them on his father's face—a plain, sallow, pock-marked face it was, in an ordinary way, but to Kit, just now, it was a countenance too truly noble to gaze on unmoved. Presently the silence was broken by a heavy kitchen chair being pushed back from the table, and then Kit stood at his father's side. He did not speak a word, nor did his father.

Their hard hands touched for a second, and they looked into each other's eyes one long questioning and answering glance. That was all. Kit returned to his place. Yes, he returned to his place, but his soul was down at Uncle Vallon's feet, and Uncle Vallon was bending over it with the blessing that he never breathed in words.

"So this is Jack Vallon, is it?" thought Humphrey to himself, at the close of the dinner, as he put the ale-glass to his lips and set it down again without drinking. Nay, Humphrey Standish, in vain you hold your glass up to the light —your good old ale is as fine and clear as ever: the evil taste is in your own mouth.

They were all silent, when Humphrey made them start by suddenly turning and resting his glass on his knee, and pointing towards the children with his pipe, while saying to his nephew—

"You'll have the kindness, Kit, you and your father, to take that there business on your own hands, seein' as I've got that on mine as keeps 'em pretty full. *You* may be able to attend to such things — you and him may be, I dare say; and it's no doubt very creditable on you; but as for me, *I* find it as much, or as I may say, *more* than I can do to manage them as belongs to me, and keep 'em from makin' fools of 'emselves, without turnin' charity lawyer for every tramp as comes trespassing on my premises. As to putting my hands in my pocket, I've no objection to that in a reasonable way, though I aint got two hundred laid by unbeknown to my family, as some folks has. My pocket and my wittles is at your service, if so be they're wanted; but responsibility aint, and there's an end on't."

As he ceased, there was a silence which seemed perfectly terrible to poor Constance. She had a feeling that she ought to get up and say something about her willingness to go away with her brother; but her tongue seemed to have lost all power of speech, and for the moment the attack, in its very suddenness and unexpectedness, quite overwhelmed her.

Uncle Vallon, having waited to see if any one else would speak before him, at last said—

"Will you tell me, my dear, where you are going, and what you want to do? Don't be afraid to speak out."

"We want, please, sir, to get to my aunt, who lives at Westcliff."

"And haven't you money enough to get there in the quickest way—by the coaches?"

"A man took it all from us, else we had enough, by walking part of the way."

"But, my dear, hadn't you better write to your aunt, and tell her where you are, before you undertake so long a journey?"

"Please to remember, Jack Vallon, what I said a bit ago," interrupted Humphrey Standish. "I don't mean to do an unkind thing, but I say, and I'll stand to it, no responsibilities for me."

"You mean, Humphrey, I suppose, you don't wish them to stay here any longer—not even while they wait for the aunt's answer?"

"*Wish* it! Humph! they shan't, and that's what I've got to say, Jack. No offence to them— or you."

Uncle Vallon seemed about to speak hurriedly

in reply, then paused and dropped his head—
a habit of his when meditating. A moment after
he heard his wife say—

"Why can't we take them home with us for
a bit? Margaret tells me she's a good, useful
girl. I want help, and we could send the boy to
school—I mean, till the letter comes."

Uncle Vallon's face brightened all over, but
there was something in his subdued manner of
speaking that implied he had been looking for
such a result, and that, now it was obtained, the
less fuss he made about the mode, the better it
would be.

"Very well, children; then get ready as soon
as you like for Peeler's Pond, for the chaise won't
hold us all, and so we must send you on first.
You take them, Kit, and then give the horse as
long a rest as you can before coming to fetch us
in the evening."

CHAPTER X.

PEELER'S POND must, to judge from its appearance, have become a village unintentionally. The large, old-fashioned farm cottage, which had first impregnated the sweet wood air with its smoke, had been joined by one quiet homestead and another until there was, at the woody foot of the hill, a very fair cluster of houses—a cluster quite considerable enough to be called a village, only that they had fitted and arranged themselves in so comfortable and picturesque a manner, and with so little destruction to the fine old trees of Peeler's Pond, that, at first sight, they rather gave one the impression of being a pic-nic party down in the woods, than of forming a real and stable little hamlet likely to hold its ground and increase with time.

The pond itself, from which the place took its

name, and which was situated in the centre of the village, was a commonplace piece of water enough, fenced round with white paling, apparently for the safety of the donkeys on the green rather than of the children, for whom there was plenty of room to run under. It may, no doubt, have been a more picturesque pond once upon a time. What common village pond now used for cooling horses' legs in, or receiving all vagrant dogs, very young kittens, or very old cats, and being, besides, the place of fashionable resort for all the ducks and geese of the neighbourhood—what village pond, though turned to these uses, does not seem, in the lull of a spring noon, or in the twilight of a summer's morning, to tell, like man's records, of a vanished paradise; to be stirred by a breath of memory so plaintive that its stunted willow and its few remaining rushes bow with one accord before it, as though yearning after that dim morning of creation ere a leaf had fallen or a flower decayed?—a time when, framed with its blue forget-me-nots, it was a fitting mirror to reflect heaven's face, in all its thousand

and ever-beautiful changes—when water-lilies may have floated on its clear bosom; when that same bare, stunted willow, which now the common little sparrows scorn to build their nests in, was a wilderness of silvery leaves, uttering a music like that which wooed poor sick Ophelia to her doom.

It will be remembered that it was a Sunday evening on which Christopher, the good wheel-wright's son, led our little adventurers to this his native village. As they issued from the narrow lane the sunset colours were fading slowly in the murky waters of the pond, round which a tribe of yellow, downy goslings were taking their last sail ere retiring for the night. Already several ducks were waddling slowly up the green towards their homes, and had stopped at different intervals on the slope, some to admire the evolutions of the little goslings in the water, others to scan the chaise and its occupants with a lazy curiosity, and—as 'Duke could not help thinking, as he saw them occasionally glance askance at one another with a slight rise of the wings, very much resembling that movement we call shrugging the shoulders—to pass satirical remarks thereon, as it stopped before a door in a high wooden fence, tarred black, with light tree-tops appearing above it.

Christopher took a large key from his pocket and proceeded to unlock the freshly-tarred door.

A very fresh and pleasant picture it opened upon, that clumsy black door—a little yard, irregularly paved with round and oval stones, which shone as snow-white this April weather as the blossoms that the old blackthorn by the pump showered down upon them. On the right was the back of Uncle Vallon's workshop, a low-roofed, ungainly building, opening towards the road which Christopher had left when he turned into the narrow lane. On the other side of the door were a stable and a gigantic old pump, with a red watering-can and some garden tools grouped round it. Directly opposite the door, and at the end of a long garden, stood the wheelwright's cottage. It was not an ideal cottage, boasted of no ancient thatched roof, or latticed windows, or rural porch; on the contrary, take it by itself, it was as unsightly as a modern cottage could well be, for the wheelwright, though an excellent man at heart, was not in any way remarkable for good taste. The garden, also, was not laid out after the style of gardens most admired. It never, for instance, boasted the elegant and intricate archwork of scarlet runners that the garden of " The Waggoner's Rest " did, where Christopher and Madgie used to play at hide-and-seek every Sunday of their lives, till Madgie went into long dresses, and preferred sitting in the parlour and eating oranges to tearing her skirts with the pea-sticks. No—Uncle Vallon's was not such a garden as his brother-in-law's at Iversham, but all that two or three hours a day of hard, loving labour, without much taste or skill, could do for it, he did. Yet, though we all know love is a great gardener, and frequently achieves wonderful things entirely unhelped by skill, he will at times plant his roses and cabbages together indiscriminately, and allow his most beautiful lilies to be choked by common

clambering peas—and so it was in Uncle Vallon's
case. The path leading straight from the yard
to the house-door was bordered with violets,
parsley, double daisies—white and red, thyme,
pansies, horseradish, and other useful, low-grow-
ing vegetables. And year by year, on each side
of this path, roses, hollyhocks, beans, dahlias,
lettuces, tiger-lilies, and sunflowers, flourished
together in sweet companionship. An elder-tree
and a lithe laburnum, arching where the path
began, formed a fitting frame for this rude garden
picture. Rude, indeed, and yet dearly cherished
in more hearts than one. Little children, out
with their nurses in the hot weather, loved it—
and would pause on the dusty road to peep at it
through the cracks in the black door. Uncle
Vallon flattered himself it was the excellent taste
displayed in the arrangement of form and colour
that these little ones paused to admire ; and he
beamed upon them as he slaked their thirst with a
drink of the delicious pump-water, lifting the red
can so gently for fear of hurting the tiny rose lips
with its sharp spout. He did not know, nor did

they, that there was a spirit pervading his garden that drew them thither as if by magic; that made them so love the gleam of the white stones, the dripping of the pump, and the sweet smell of the flowers, that in years to come they would remember the glimpses through that door as tenderly and wonderingly as if they had been glimpses of paradise; and those rose lips, withered by their long and bitter draught of life, would thirst in vain for a nectar as delicious as the water from that old red can. What spirit was it, then? What but the sweet spirit of loving-kindness? Our little Poplar felt it as she crossed the yard with Christopher, and passed under the rustic arch into the garden; it entered her heart with the soft beauty and stillness of the Sabbath evening, and beckoned her across the threshold of the cottage-door, whispering — " Here, for awhile, rest."

Simple and insignificant as the events of the Sunday may have appeared to the reader, they tended, nevertheless, to change greatly the aspect of affairs in the wheelwright's quiet household. The only subject discussed at breakfast next norning was that which naturally lay nearest the father's and mother's heart, namely, Christopher.

" Of course, Eppie," said the wheelwright, in a tone of resignation, " when he's gone to live at the works at Todness, we mustn't expect to have him home here oftener than once a week; he *might* come over of evenings once in a way; but if he attends to his business, and reads himself up a bit—for look you here, my boy," said Mr. Vallon, pushing his cup from him, and folding his brawny hands on the table, " a bit of learning in a man's head is like a pool o' water in a meadow; while there's more running into it, though it's ever so little, it'll keep good and fresh; but leave it shut in to itself, and it'll get stagnated and unwholesome, and breed all sorts o' disorders and unnatural things. So, as I was saying, Eppie, if he does as he ought— reads himself up a bit at the Institootion yonder, in his spare hours, why, I take it, he'll have enough to do all the week, without walking over here a good six mile; but as to Sundays, my lad, you know my opinion on them, and I know you won't cross me in it; it's the only thing I've got to ask of you, Kit, now you're a-starting in life, is that you'll come home every Sunday. Perhaps I've got too strong notions on that matter; but I mean to bide by 'em. It's my opinion a lad can't well go wrong so long as he comes home of a Sunday. I'd even go so far as to say that if the Old Gentleman himself, supposin' he was once a lad beginning the world, had been made to spend his Sundays at home, he'd never 'a' been what he is."

Kit laughed, but gave his sacred promise to adhere to this simple talisman, which, by his father's account, might have wrought so wondrous and desirable a difference in the state of humanity in general. He then ventured to inquire how the little quarrel with his uncle Humphrey had terminated.

"My boy," answered the wheelwright, "your grandfather did it all with his fiddle, for which

I am sure we are greatly beholden to him; for your uncle is your uncle, Kit, whatever his notions may be; and I'm a'most as much again' falling out with your own flesh and blood, as I am again' spending your Sundays away from home; and so you see, Christopher, we're much beholden to your grandfather for setting things to rights with his fiddle."

Christopher did not fail to make his acknowledgments to his grandfather, who stood at the door, with a pewter pot that flashed in the sunshine, waiting for his breakfast ale, blushing all over his bald head as he listened to these praises of his musical genius, and mumbling, "Not at all, not at all."

How grandfather Vallon "set things right with his fiddle" Constance had more than one opportunity of seeing that day. Whenever the conversation seemed likely to grow into a heated discussion, grandfather immediately raised his eyes to the shelf whereon his fiddle lay, and approaching it on tiptoe, took it down and began playing away vigorously, eyeing the disputants meanwhile with the air of a doctor who is administering some dangerously powerful restorative; and after listening awhile to the strains, though they were by no means harmonious or soothing, the wheelwright invariably gave up his part in the discussion, and said apologetically,—

"Thank you, father, thank you; we've recollected ourselves."

The meal over, the wheelwright donned his apron, kissed the baby, and went to work. Grandfather Vallon also encased his thin, long figure in a leather apron, that made him look like a white-headed bodkin in a sheath, and sallied forth to the workshop with a grave, business-like air; though he did little else in it but grind tools for his son, help him with his lunch ale, and occasionally play him a tune on the fiddle. As to Christopher, half an hour later found him melting glue over the fire, superintending the cutting-out of his new collars, and watching, with an odd mingling of curiosity, amusement, and suspicion, a certain little figure bending, with a perplexed and weary face, over a sheet of writing-paper, as yet unsullied by the touch of the pen held over it. What manner of child or woman (for there was as much of the one as the other in her) could this be whom he had snatched from the most terrible of death's ministers? And what was that sad, un-flinching purpose, mysterious, inexplicable, from which she never seemed to withdraw those steady, mournful eyes, or cease to follow with those firm, but weary feet? Was it for good or for evil?—selfish, or self-sacrificing? He remembered how he had actually asked her, that night down by the river, to confide her secret to him, and how she had refused, with a good deal of vexation; and he smiled to himself as he thought how little trouble it would be to him to find it out, if he chose to do so. Meantime, he had done his best to place their position in as reasonable and satisfactory a light as he could to his father and mother.

While Kit was stirring his glue, and making his reflections upon her thus, Constance, bending over that blank sheet of paper, was calling to her mind a scene that took place some seven or eight years back, in a darkened room of the old house at Aberford, and where she had seen for a few minutes the person to whom she was now trying to write—her mother's sister.

Leaning her cheek on her hand, and looking down at the paper, she seemed to see a form stretched upon a bed, and a face with liquid, spiritual eyes, lifting itself heavenward from masses of black tangled hair, which the hands were tearing in the last agonies of death. One —a man—sat in a chair at the foot of the bed, with a white, unrumpled handkerchief to his eyes; another—a woman—also knelt beside the bed, with a face and form wonderfully resembling the face and form of the dying. Then it seemed to Constance the face sank down on the dishevelled hair, and lay there at perfect rest, so mobile, so beautiful, that the room was no more dark; and ere long the figure crouching by the bedside arose, and Constance beheld a lady, tall and slender, like her mother, but, unlike her,

showing pride and stateliness in every gesture.
Moving to the foot of the bed, she turned eyes,
full of passionate, vengeful grief, upon him who
sat there with his white handkerchief to his face,
and, pointing to the quiet form upon the bed,
uttered words of bitter reproach. Then Constance remembered being caught up and held
tightly in her arms, and wept over, and intreated
and commanded, in a confused, passionate flow
of words—not one of which she could recal—to
come to her in any trouble, and she should find
in her a mother.

The dark room and all within it vanished, but
the vision had done its work; the pen flew over
the paper fast—so fast as to perfectly astonish
Kit, and yet not so fast as the loving, pleading
words came gushing from the heart that had at
last opened fully and unrestrainedly at memory's
touch. Here, surely, she felt, was a love strong
enough to pity and help her, without trying to
force from her that one secret which she must
bear unrevealed to the end of life. She ran on
about 'Duke, her love and her fear for him, and

her great wish to get him to school, till the whole sheet was filled with her round school-hand, and Christopher quietly, and, as he thought, unseen, laid another near her; but she looked up and smiled sweetly and wonderingly, as one to whom anything in the shape of courtesy is strange, as she said—" Thank you, it is done."

" Is it?" said Christopher. " You'd better let me give it to grandfather, then, to go up the road and watch for the mail passing; he's got nothing else to do but fidget for his beer."

" There, then—wish it luck for us, Christopher."

One evening the wheelwright was at work in his garden. Three days of incessant rain had passed, during which the variegated border of flowers and vegetables before spoken of had grown at such a rate as to considerably narrow the path, and the young spring annuals were pricking up crisp and strong, and sending forth such long trailing shoots as quite baffled the wheelwright's skill in training, and made him glad of the assis-

tance of those expert little brown hands that
worked beside him. During two of these days,
Constance had been watching for an answer to
her letter, about which all the family had shown
nearly as much anxiety as herself. Old Grandfather Vallon would put down his fiddle, or even
his beer, to look questioningly at Christopher,
when he returned from his visits to the post-office,
and say, " Tut ! tut !" when Kit shook his
head.

Kit had gone to the post-office this evening,
and Constance, suddenly turning her head as she
worked in the garden, saw him standing there
with a letter in his hand. How she walked up
the garden and into the house she scarcely knew ;
for now, as she stood in her little bedroom, her
knees would not support her, and she had to
kneel down and press her hands tightly to her
side for some seconds before she could open the
letter and discover her fate.

The tiny window, with its coarse calico
curtains, admitted just enough of the tender
April twilight to enable her to read it.

"MY DEAR NIECE,

"I am very much surprised to hear of the strange step you have just taken, and it is only a long knowledge of your father that keeps me from strongly urging you to return. I am now too unwell to inquire into your affairs, but shall do so as soon as I get stronger; in the meantime the request you make for your brother is so simple and clear, that I have no hesitation in granting it. I shall at once communicate with John Vallon, the wheelwright, whom I know to be a most trustworthy man, and arrange all money matters with him. So place your brother at school as soon as you like. There is one on the Downs, near you—Summerfield's academy, Plantagenet House — which I can recommend highly. With wishes for your welfare,

"I am, my dear niece,

"Your affectionate aunt,

"JANE ARMSTRONG."

Constance read her letter twice over, and cold, proud, and distant as its tone was, she rose to her feet with the elasticity of one who, travelling in the darkness, suddenly sees a light defining clearly the path she has been seeking. No longer was the aim of her heart a dim, hopeless thing, to be attained only by a hurrying on of weary little feet through the strange world, further and further away from where that heart so longed to rest. The blind impulse had become a possibility. The aim was to be won by work. The thought gave her wonderful strength—such strength that she felt, if needs be, rather than flinch from her purpose, she could and would meet *him*, and give him again her sad, firm challenge as she had done on that spring morning when he overtook them by the Plague-Stone at the beginning of their pilgrimage. She sat thinking, with her elbows fixed on the broad window-sill, till it grew too dark to see the glimmer of the yard pavement through the trees; and then, taking her letter, she found her way down-stairs and into the parlour, where the wheelwright's family had assembled for the evening.

She slipped quietly in and sat down by Mrs.

Vallon. Every one was anxious, yet every one forbore to question her concerning the letter she held. The room was silent for some minutes, except, indeed, that now and then Grandfather Vallon, who sat mending his fiddle, with his tools on a tea-tray, would make his chair creak and startle the baby, and draw upon himself a warning gaze from the brown eyes of his daughter-in-law, or perhaps let one of his tools fall on the table, and make the wheelwright say, reproachfully—" Have a care, father! have a care! He wants a bigger teaboard, Eppie." And Eppie would frown, and raise her eyebrows, and say she " hadn't patience!" Poor Mrs. Vallon, she had a sweet temper, but that sweet temper was sorely tried by her father-in-law, and the wheelwright had often much ado in keeping their warfare from destroying his domestic peace. He could have provided for the old gentleman elsewhere, but wisely reflecting that every woman, even one as sweet-tempered as his wife, " must let out her spirit on somebody," and that no one would have borne it so quietly as his father, he came to the conclusion that things had best remain as they were.

"Am I to read it out, my dear?" asked the wheelwright, as Constance put the letter in his hand.

"If you please, Uncle Vallon," said she, for uncle was the name by which he had taught his little guests to call him.

And Uncle Vallon took the letter and read it slowly and feelingly, while Christopher laid down his book, and grandfather paused with his spectacles on his nose to listen. After the reading of the letter a silence ensued, which was broken by grandfather's remarking it was "werry deep"— his usual verdict to anything he could not understand, or that sounded rather dreary.

"There, the sooner you get him rigged out, my dear, the better," said the wheelwright, though to judge by the manner in which he patted 'Duke's head, he was in no violent hurry to get rid of him.

After a long discussion between Mrs. Vallon and Constance, carried on in whispers under fear of grandfather's fiddle, it was decided that 'Duke could not go until after the midsummer holidays; a most satisfactory conclusion to him, for life at Peeler's Pond in the bird-nesting season was not to be given up without a pang.

Mrs. Vallon then went into the kitchen to lay the cloth for supper, calling grandfather after her; and Kit and his father filled and lighted their pipes, and went for a turn in the garden, that the two children might be alone to talk over their changed fortunes.

But it was Constance alone who talked. With 'Duke's head in her lap, she twined the curls that shone like gold in the firelight round and round her fingers, and, while her heart was faint and sick at parting from what alone made her exile endurable, she spoke with such a strong, hopeful voice in the child's ear, that his face began to flush, and his blue eyes to kindle, as he listened.

When the day of parting came round, sooner than it was wanted, as most days of parting do, it required all uncle Vallon's tender philosophy, and all grandfather's musical powers, to keep the children in good heart and fit them for their ordeal.

Up to the very last second that 'Duke was with her, Constance kept a smiling face and dry eyes, but when he had gone, when Mrs. Vallon stuffed the baby in her arms to distract her thoughts, and grandfather began to play, her heart seemed suddenly to sink within her, and, laying the baby back in its crib, she ran out down the garden, and across the little stone yard, now all fragrant with clematis, and leaning against the black, tarred door, strained her eyes through the red light of the sunset for a last glimpse of him.

There lay the little valley flooded in the warmth and sparkle of the midsummer day. So wild and desolate an air enveloped the surrounding hills, that, as the valley flashed upon the sight, in all its freshness and high cultivation, it reminded one of those visionary pictures of sea and air, which mariners sometimes mistake for land, and which fade as they try to approach them. The river flowed clear and strong between fields of long grass purple with clover, and under dark, high trees that here and there almost met across it. The little woods were, as yet, masses of rich dark green, untouched by yellow, and the whole valley, stretching out in its summer brilliancy and fulness, was like a splendid garden. It was a picture that would remain with her always, not for its own sake, but because it enclosed that little insignificant figure which walked last of a long file of boys winding slowly up the gorse-covered hill.

That same evening, as the bells of Aberford Minster chimed away the daylight softly and tenderly, an old man sat musing on the Plague-Stone.

The place retained but little of the beauty it had worn in spring-time, for the heath was dry and sunburnt, the hawthorns were recovering their look of weird old age; the little brook was still and sad, and under its clear water, dull, mud-coloured foliage waved with a slow and deathly motion. But in vivid and wonderful contrast to all this dreariness, there had sprung

from a crack in the flags that formed the base-
ment floor of the old Plague-Stone, one flower, a
foxglove of rare and perfect beauty, that seemed
waving with all the grace, and glowing with all
the tints of an Eastern summer. It was over this
the solitary man was pondering, as if wondering
how such a thing could blossom from a stone.
Very often did he come there now at the close of
those sultry days, for home was not what it used
once to be. No linnet sang in the dark parlour
window, the very grape-vine forbore putting forth
its few pale leaves this summer; but what moved
him most, and filled him with all kinds of vague
fancies and terrors, was that the dark old house
seemed smitten from garret to base with decay
and uncleanliness. Now that the quiet, busy
little form which used to move about it like a
spirit of purity and health had passed away, it
seemed as if it must inevitably rot and crumble
panel by panel and stair by stair until the roof
fell. Throughout the day while busy in the shop
he was cheerful enough, and retained all his old
pleasantness of manner; it was when the dusky

evening crept on, and the cold, holy stars looked down upon him, and the shadow of the Minster wall fell upon his house front like a frown, when the beetles came in black, gleaming troops up the sloping parlour floor, and the shrill-voiced crickets leaped about the empty parlour grate, it was then that the dark fancies seized upon him and held him to his chair for long hours together, or made him flee from the house as if pursued.

At such times he nearly always bent his trembling, uncertain steps across the path towards the old Plague-Stone; and there sat until the fresh heath air and solitude quieted his brain, and brought a healthier, though deeper sadness, over him. It was strange the comfort and vague dim promise that stone seemed to contain for him, in his darkest moments. One little blossom that changed with the months invariably greeted him, wafting him its perfume as he came across the heath, or waving near the stone with mysterious and suggestive beauty. The Plague-Stone indeed seemed the only point from which he could still hold a kind of far-off sorrowful communion with his children, while maintaining satisfactorily his position towards his fellow-men. Sometimes he felt as if the little wanderers, too, visited it and thought of him, and perhaps left him that never-failing blossom there as a token that they loved him still; and it often seemed to him that if ever he should clasp his boy to his heart again with the pride of an unreproachful and pure conscience, it would be at the grey old Plague-Stone. Time after time, while giving himself up to such ima-ginings as these, was he moved to press his hands over his ears to shut out the Minster bells, which seemed to take the voices of his children, and call to him to cast from him that numbing fear of his fellow-men, to take up the beautiful shame of repentance and follow them.

Still as yet that repentance, in spite of all he suffered, was but a garment fluttering near him in a dream; he saw it, half-longed for it; but ever the fear of what it would reveal to men did he seize and wear it openly, held his hand paralysed.

So time passed on, week followed week, and

the foxglove by the Plague-Stone shrivelled away,
and a white convolvulus came in its place; month
followed month, and the primroses were there
again; year followed year, and still he lived his
two lives—the guilty, suffering, but unrepentant
father, and the honoured townsman of Aberford.

CHAPTER XI.

" Ay, it's his whistle, sure enough, old woman," said the wheelwright, as, some five years later than the period referred to in the last chapter, they all stood at the door peering down through the darkness; " it's Kit's whistle, but I'm hanged if I knew the cut of him in that dandified coat! Grandfather! " he shouted, putting his head in at the door, and making a speaking-trumpet of his hands, " be so good as to set the light in the winder. Here he is ! "

There was a whining answer from within, half of joy, half of complaint, and a blundering foot-step across the room, but no light appeared at the window.

"Is he come? Is Christopher come? Oh, where is the light? How can I find the light,

Jack?—you're always forgetting I'm blind! O dear! O dear! where is it?"

The wheelwright drew his sleeve across his eyes, and muttered, "So I am, poor soul," then shouted in at the door, "Never mind, father, sit ye still. He aint forgot the way, I'll lay a wager."

But one of the group quietly glided into the house, asking herself whether Christopher would care to see her awaiting him like one of the family—she, a stranger under his father's roof. So she came in, and set the candle in the window, and led the old man back to his seat and sat down beside him, listening, with him, for that well-known footstep. Meanwhile, before Christopher comes up the garden, we may as well mention two facts, which the flickering light in the window reveals. First, then, looking in at the little window, it is perceptible that the supper, though it is to celebrate Kit's return for Christmas, is a sadly frugal one; and, moreover, the same light, zigzagging faintly down the garden, discovers to us a door flung back on its hinges and an empty stable.

"Jack Vallon," the wheelwright's brother-in-law had said to him, as a last warning against lifting his son above his "proper station," "do this thing, and, mark my words, you'll come to want. He'll be always a-suckin' and a-suckin' of you like a leech, and your little bit o' money 'll go like butter afore the sun. Set a chap half-way up a hill, an' it stands to reason as he'll make for the top, an' the higher he gets the more balance he wants. Draw back while there's time, Jack, and I'll help you to knock this thing out of his head and set his mind on something else; or go on, and, mark my words, you'll come to want."

Jack Vallon had gone on—had, through heavy expenses on Christopher's account, come to want; yet he did not regret it, and smiled contentedly while Humphrey Standish crowed over him, answering, "Let us wait and see."

Christopher's apprenticeship had been up half a year, during which time he had been employed in London on an experiment likely to prove of great importance to him, as well as to his employers, if successful. After long suspense, there had come, this Christmas week, a letter from Kit, which brought new life to the wheelwright, and made him exult in all the hardships to which he had exposed himself for his boy's sake, and which sent Mrs. Vallon off by coach to "The Waggoner's Rest" in such a transport of pride that she knew not what she was about; and was reminded by Mrs. Standish, in the midst of her eulogy on Kit, that she had put her best cap on over her old one. It was unanimously agreed that Christopher was to know nothing of the sacrifices that had been made at home for him, save those which were obvious, as in the case of Tommy's disappearance. "It 'ud be hard, you know, Eppie, for the lad, now he's got a bit o' money, to be fancyin' it his duty to make us returns; so let's keep things as smooth as we can while he's here," the wheel-wright said, "and we'll draw in again when he's gone. There's the old watch and the blunderbuss still, you know; and, if all comes to all, why, there's such a thing as letting the place and going into two rooms; but don't grizzle—that's far off yet, thank God."

The whistle stopped as the footsteps came up the garden, quickening to a run; and, in another instant, a lot of bags and parcels were cast down on the doorstep, and Kit's poor, worn mother was crying on her boy's shoulder; and, in spite of the wheelwright's warning nudge, was pouring into his ear a torrent of miseries.

"My boy! my boy! so he's really come home! And you mustn't be ashamed of us, Kit dear, if you find things different to what you've bin used to; I don't say as it's your fault, dear, because I know your father's never let you know anything about it; but it's bin such a time with us, Kit—with me, at least. Your father—bless him!—he never feels nothing, and I do my best, God knows, to keep that from him; but it's me it all falls on, Kit; and the time I've had of it there's no tongue can tell—trouble on trouble. There's your little brother Georgy, as good a child as ever was born, so far as morals go, but always in the dirt, or tormenting of his grandfather; and there's

him, poor soul, getting more and more of a baby
every day of his life; and Georgy's ruined his
fiddle, and he can't see to mend it, and sits
cryin' over it so as you never saw the like. And
O dear! O dear! what's to become on us God
A'mighty only knows!"

"Come, come, Eppie, there's time enough for
talking over troubles," said the wheelwright,
gently unclasping her hands to free Kit. "Come,
come into the light, my man, and let's see
what six months of town life has done for
you."

They picked up the carpet-bags and parcels
from the door-step and entered the kitchen, now
cheery enough with bright household things and
a hissing fire.

"Upon my soul I shouldn't have known
him!" cried the wheelwright, never ceasing to
shake Kit's hand as he examined him from head
to foot. "Is *this* the style of coat they're wearing now, my boy? Bless my soul!"

Christopher's roar of laughter at his father's
astonishment was broken in upon by a cry from

poor old Grandfather Vallon, who was fumbling across the room to get to him.

"Why, what's the matter, grandfather?" said Kit, laying his hands on his shoulders and looking into his face, startled to see his eyes staring right beyond him. "Father, what's the matter?"

The wheelwright shook his head and turned away, and the old man clung about his grandson, sobbing like a child.

"I can't see you, Christopher; I'm blind, my boy—stone blind. Oh, what shall I do? I want to see him so! Let me see him! Christopher! Christopher!"

Christopher pushed him from him and burst into tears. Out in the world they called him somewhat hard and impenetrable, and it is true his nature was not one to be easily moved; but this cry, this helpless cry, of Grandfather Vallon penetrated to his very marrow, and hurt him like a sword-thrust. He led the long, trembling, clinging figure to the arm-chair, and silently and almost tenderly seated it, while the old man still kept crying out that he wanted to see him—he must see him.

"Come, grandfather," said Kit, as soon as he could speak, "let me unpack the present I've got for you, and while I'm doing it see if you can guess what it is."

"What does he say?" asked the old man of his son while Kit was busy unpacking a huge parcel. The wheelwright applied his hands to his ears as a speaking-trumpet again, and shouted, loud enough to be heard out on the green—

"He says he's got a present for you, worth having, you know. Come all the way from London."

"Eh, a present? What's the use of it to me? Take it away, lad—I can't see it. Take it away."

"Ay, but you *can* hear it, grandfather. Look here: put it against you, so. Now take this in your other hand—there! Now do you know what it is?"

The trembling hand with the violin stick fell to work; the deadened sense of the ear quickened at the loved sounds; and the poor, weary heart woke from its stupor. He played one of his favourite old airs carefully through, and then sat down and felt his new treasure all over, with tears streaming down his cheeks the while.

"Did you ever see such a lad?" shouted the wheelwright through his hands. "And he's come back such a gentleman! I didn't know his cut myself at first."

"I always said as he'd be a gentleman, I did," answered Grandfather Vallon, with a touch of pride in his piping voice; "I've said so ever since he used to make me go down on my knees to be his horse, and ride on me like a lord markiss, haven't I, Eppie? Ah, my boy, you've done me good. How come you to think on your poor, good-for-nothing old grandfather up at London? But he's done me good, Jack; and I'll try and not be a worrit to Eppie while it pleases God A'mighty to spare me."

"Now don't go to talk i' that way, grandfather, don't," said Eppie. "Worrit, indeed! Why, what should we all do without you?"

While the two were hanging about the old man,

comforting him and describing to him the beautiful appearance of the violin, Christopher looked round the dear old place with a vague presentiment of discovering more sad changes. But no; such changes as had really taken place had been carefully concealed to-night. The quiet little figure sitting in the gloom by the clock-case waited for the bright, roving brown eyes to turn her way. They were some time before they reached that corner, so that she had opportunity of judging for herself of the talked-of change in Christopher's appearance.

That this last year or two had been different to every other year of Christopher's life it was easy to perceive. The lax, easy expression of the mouth, and the confident glance, had given place to a look of slight uncertainty and calm observance. The lesson had, without doubt, been many times repeated for him, that he, like other men, could only win the success that he had once looked upon as a free gift of Providence by constant struggle, and with the best years of his life. But there was also that in his face which declared that he had accepted it at that price; that on no account would he let it pass from him—a calm, firm courage, which none but eyes such as Constance's, which knew him well, could have perceived. To others, the change in Christopher's face would seem by no means an improvement; for all that bright, fearless gaiety which had made his presence have the effect of a wild, sunny March day on the spirits, and gave an impression of his being remarkably handsome, had entirely disappeared; and now he could be taken for nothing more than a well-built, agreeable young fellow—gentlemanly, because so perfectly unaffected, easy, and self-sustained.

Constance was still looking at him and wondering whether his face had lost or gained most, and rather inclining to decide on the former, when the roving eyes met her own, and lighted up with recognition.

"Christopher!"

She had started forward to meet him the instant their eyes met. Christopher clasped the little brown hand and smiled; and while the clasp and the smile lasted, Constance said joyfully within herself, " He is the same—the very same." For often had she shaken her head as she sat at her close, wearying work, and said to herself, " This Christopher, this good friend who has done so much for you, and whose return you look forward to with more pleasure than you have known for years, is, ten chances to one, long ere this dead to you, and one will return in his place with whom you can have nothing in common."

But this glow of friendly confidence was of brief duration, for Christopher had hardly touched her hand than he let it go again, and the smile seemed to vanish under the shade of some unpleasant recollection.

" Is the parlour open to the public to-night ? " he asked the wheelwright as he took a candle from the table ; " because I've some news for Miss Chorley, and if it is we'll go in there, and I'll deliver it up before supper." It must here be mentioned of the wheelwright that though, during the day-time, he had for years been accustomed to leave all the members of his family pretty

much to their own devices, he had been exceedingly particular that the evening should find
them in as high a state of civilisation as was
compatible with existing circumstances. The parlour used to be kept under lock and key all day;
but in the evening, when he came in from his
gardening, the wheelwright, divesting himself of
his boots outside the door, would unlock it himself, and place a bouquet of fresh flowers on the
polished table, light the oil-lamp, and take down
a well-bound book or two from the bookshelf of
stained deal which Kit had made, and distribute
them about the room. There had been a time
when the parlour was pervaded by the light of
two golden heads, and the prattling of two little
tongues; and the wheelwright had then often
fancied himself in a land of beauty and music
such as Christopher sometimes read of in the
Eastern tales. When these heads, and all the
hopes with which he had encompassed them, as
he watched them, week by week, rising a little
higher than the table, were laid to rest in the
cold earth, the parlour had been shut up for a while.

But it was not many days before the wheelwright's boots were seen outside the door again, and his fresh flowers on the table; for, as the patriarchs of old made acknowledgment of the mercy of their God towards them by sacrifices more or less costly, so it had ever been his wont to make this room a shrine on which to display, in humble gratitude, the extent of his prosperity.

And now again the parlour had been long closed. But as Kit spoke, the wheelwright rose and set about unlocking it with great alacrity; yet, owing to two or three little alterations he had to arrange ere it could be seen by Christopher—such as placing some books in the gap on the mantelpiece left by the disappearance of the pretty bronze timepiece, and filling up sundry other vacancies—owing, I say, to this, it was several minutes before he returned, flustered and blushing at the deception he was practising, and announced that the parlour was at Kit's service.

Constance had remained still just where Christopher had dropped her hand, and now she followed him into the parlour mechanically, and stood resting one hand on the table, listening for his first words with a patient, stony kind of dread on her face.

"I dare say you guess what it is?" Christopher said with his old bluntness.

"Has it come at last, then?—have you seen him?" she asked, almost inaudibly, but calmly, as if prepared for anything.

"No, I have not; but he is at Todness, and I found this at my lodgings to-night, inclosed in an envelope addressed to me."

She took the letter from him, and, as she read the words, "To be forwarded to Miss Constance Chorley," started, for the familiar hand seemed to bring the writer suddenly and vividly before her.

"Sit down," said Christopher, pushing her a chair. "Shall I go or stay while you read it?"

"Stay, Christopher, if you please," she answered, dropping into the chair.

She broke the black seal quickly, drew out the letter, and began to read it with compressed lips, and eyes that seemed prepared to take in unflinchingly anything that might await them. The first closely-written sheet was read through and turned before Christopher saw any change in the resolute face, which he watched narrowly; but the eyes had not traversed many lines of the next before they began to fill, and the firm mouth to quiver at the corners. For a few seconds she was blinded and could not go on; but, after letting the tears flow quietly down, pattering on the letter, she held it nearer the candle, and continued to read from the line where she had left off, and from which we will follow her.

"But all I have written, Constance, cannot convey to you an idea of what I suffer hourly, day and night. I feel as if I already knew the loneliness of the grave, and often pray to the Almighty to give me the unconsciousness of the grave also. I do not say but that some in this cold world have shown me great kindness, but how can the kindness of strangers be anything but gall and wormwood to me when I remember that my own child has withdrawn herself from me, as not being worthy to breathe the same air with her? O Constance, dear Constance, re-

member my age and my helplessness! You will,
I know, have pity, and return to one who feels
the great need he has of his children, and of the
comfort of their presence. Yes, you will come,
I feel assured. You will get this to-night, and
to-night you will come to the address enclosed,
where you will find a woman who will bring you
to me. Do not be surprised or startled at any
condition you may find me in. Again I say,
I am waiting.—Your miserable father,

" D. C."

Christopher, I think, would hardly have liked
to remain in the room could he have guessed how
every word of that letter would pierce the young
heart whose timidity and strength of love in
leaving her home he had once mistaken for
hardness.

When she had read the last word, the letter
dropped on to the floor, and she sat with her
hands clasped in her lap, a picture of white, dry-
eyed misery. Was it remorse, or what? Christopher asked himself, as he watched her motionless, silent figure minute after minute; but

whatever it might be, he saw that she must needs be roused; and, after hunting about for something to say as commonplace as the circumstances would admit, observed—

"I was afraid I was bringing you bad news, for I heard, where I stopped for a few minutes on my way from London, that Mr. Chorley had left Aberford, and that the old place was all shut up: I could not learn why from the person who told me."

Constance evidently had not taken in the sense of his words, but his voice seemed to awaken her from her trance of grief. She lifted her arms as a child does in pain, and then let them fall heavily on the table, clasping her hands together.

"Christopher, I must go to him—I must go now directly. Where am I to go? Where is the letter?"

She took it up from the floor, looked at the address endorsed, "Weaver's Cottages, Todness," and then as she glanced hurriedly over it and her eyes fell upon the words, "Do not be surprised at any condition you may find me in," a fresh spasm of pain flitted over her face, and, turning to Christopher, she said—

" Tell me, please, Christopher, how I am to get to Todness to-night."

" Well, certainly we shall have to walk there," he returned. " There is no alternative, if you must go to-night."

" *We*, Christopher? But you are not going? Oh, no, let me go alone."

" If you wish to lose your way and arrive there some time to-morrow, go alone; but if you have any thoughts of getting there to-night, you had better let father or me go with you."

" But to take you away from them this evening! No, no. Please, Christopher, tell me all about it, and let me go by myself."

Christopher said no more, but went out into the kitchen. When Constance came down-stairs a few minutes afterwards, with her cloak and bonnet on, she found him waiting for her.

" I've explained it all to them," he said, " so you need only just go in and wish them good-bye."

And she did so, holding her hand out to each with a beseeching gaze, that seemed to say, as plainly as words could, " Please do not speak to me."

" Good-bye, my lass," said the wheelwright; " I was going to say and I hope it's only for the present; but I don't know that I ought."

Mrs. Vallon cried a little, and said as soon as ever she had a blessin' it was took away from her; and Grandfather Vallon complained that he didn't a bit know what was going on—nobody took the trouble to explain anything to him, though he was sure he wasn't so very deaf, let them say what they liked.

The leave-takings were over, the door closed after them; and, while Christopher was unlocking the high black door at the end of the garden, Constance turned to throw a hurried farewell look on the spot which had been her home for so long. For the moment she scarcely had a feeling of regret, her heart being taken up with the engrossing desire to reach her father; but years afterwards, as, with swimming eyes, she recalled that wintry

little picture of the cottage set in the white
garden, with the lights glimmering through the
leafless trees that rose high above the roof, and
stood against the cold, brilliant sky like delicate,
fantastic pencilling, she felt that, had she dreamt
of all that awaited her beyond that door, in her
deep thankfulness for the interval of peace that
the wheelwright's roof had afforded her, she must
have stooped and kissed the little white yard-
stones as she crossed them.

"Come," said Christopher, "it's a splendid
night, and we shall be able to go along
over the cliffs when we get beyond Fairleigh,
and so save three-quarters of a mile. It'll
be a little slippery, but I've got my stick,
you see. Now, Merrylegs, don't wake all the
parish."

And so, as they crossed the green, Christopher
contrived, with his old adroitness, to turn into
quite a commonplace matter-of-fact occurrence
what in most cases would have been an awkward
and peculiar one; and Constance walked along
at his side, finding comfort and strength in his

presence; and listening with a vague pleasure to the sound of his voice, but scarcely understanding a word he said, for in her heart was but one thought, one speculation — her father. How should she find him? How would he receive her?

CHAPTER XII.

THE three old churches of Todness were clanging forth a late hour of the night when Constance, Christopher, and Merrylegs came within sight of the town.

Now, to look down upon Todness from where they stood—namely, the cliff flanking it on the east—is, under any aspect, to look upon as fair a picture as can be found from beginning to end of the Borrockshire coast: but on this brilliant winter's night, when the moonlight came dazzling down upon the snow-covered cliffs that rose on each side of the town; on the snow-covered meadows which went sloping up behind the town ; on the foam-bordered sea, that roared and sucked the beach in front of the town ; and on the town itself, blinking with its Saturday night

lights, and all wet and glistening under a thaw;
on this same winter's night, it was a sight well
worth such a journey as our friends on the east
cliff had had, to behold. Not that the town
itself could lay claim to more beauty or stateliness than the most weather-beaten of tars who
rolled up and down its narrow, bustling streets
from morn till night, with hat-ribbons and
trowser-bottoms fluttering in the wind. To say
truth, indeed, Todness partook much of the aspect
of these worthies. Like theirs, its original com-
plexion had long ago been blotted out by the
sun and wind and sea passions; like them, too,
it seemed to have strange ideas of proportions,
squeezing itself in where it should be wide, and
letting itself out where it should be narrowed
off. Yet, withal, one could not find fault with
the old place, any more than with these good-
humoured salt-water veterans whom it so much
resembled—not only in its rollicking ungainliness
and self-assertion, but also in its air of hale
maritime freshness.

"If I'm not mistaken," said Christopher, as

they descended the hill, "Weaver's Cottages are somewhere in the fishing-place down there."

"Yes," answered Constance under her breath, "this is the place."

"And there's your guide!" exclaimed Kit.

A woman advanced from the door of one of a row of trim, small cottages, faced with rough stones, that glistened darkly as the snow rolled off and fell in heaps upon the little gardens, and said, "Miss Chorley, I believe?"

Constance bent her head in answer, and then with a sickening dread toiled after her guide. Street after street, court after court, was entered and left behind, until at last she found they had altogether quitted the old town, and were walking on the magnificent esplanade of St. Clement's, and her courage sank still more at the sight of the apparently endless line of cold, stately houses to be passed ere they could come upon any roof humble enough to harbour Daniel Chorley.

The cold was intense. The snow, which at Todness could not keep its place on the comfortable, warm old houses, here clothed the broad, desolate parade from end to end, clung to the stone-work of the tall mansions, and lay even on the beach, mingling with the foam of the in-coming tide, and making the expanse of surging waters more intensely black.

Constance was just wrapping her little grey cloak more closely round her, and trying not to see the distance she thought she had still to go, when her guide stopped :—

"Now, miss, this is the house."

Constance put up her veil and looked at it. It stood apart from the straight line, a little back—a solid, square house, the oldest in St. Clement's. A lawn sloped from the ground-windows to the low stone wall outside of which they stood. The roof formed a terrace command-ing all the splendid sweep of country behind, and sea before. A tall tree, draped in snow, stood making ghostly motions on each side of the square portico. From the three centre windows, and from the glass over the door, a brilliant light was streaming.

Just these points Constance noticed in the

confused glance she turned upon the house, then hastily laid her hand upon the woman's arm as she raised it towards the bell, saying, in a trembling voice, more to herself than to her guide—

" This is wrong. It is not here. I am sure it is not here ! "

The guide pulled the bell, and then turned and stared at Constance leisurely from head to foot. Constance bit her lip, and endeavoured to conceal the strange flutter that had come over her, to prepare herself to take, calmly and without surprise, whatever might come next, and to convince herself it was all a mistake.

The door was opened quickly; and a liveried footman, with a key in his hand, cautiously descended the slippery steps. Constance looked at him wistfully, in the hope of finding in his face some index to this fresh page of strange events.

The gate was unlocked, the guide had gone, and Constance was following the footman up the steps, who said, in an inquisitive manner—

" Master expects you, I believe ? "

But Constance did not answer. She followed

the man up-stairs, passing handsome windows
through which the moonlight entered like many-
coloured fluids—passing them without wonder,
without interest, for her head was giddy with the
sudden change from cold to heat, and the only
feeling she had was a longing for the mistake to
be over—a longing to be out in the cold again,
searching for the humble place where *he* lay in
sickness and in trouble.

Suddenly a door was opened before her. The
warm air and bright light of a drawing-room fell
upon her face. She was shrinking back, when
her eyes discerned a form which held her on the
threshold.

It was her father.

Mr. Chorley was alone in the drawing-room.
He was seated in an arm-chair before the fire,
and had not heard or seen her enter, for the
servant had opened the door noiselessly, and
glided down-stairs again without announcing her.

It was strange, but during those few seconds
she stood watching him, Constance felt all her
bewilderment and dizziness vanish, and her brain

seemed to grow suddenly calm and keen, so that she could hold every emotion in control whilst she looked and judged.

It has already been mentioned that a fresh and gentlemanly toilette had always been looked upon by Mr. Daniel Chorley as one of the great necesities of life; and that, even under most adverse circumstances, he had managed to maintain so respectable an appearance as to gain for himself the appellation of "the old gentleman." Now, therefore, there could be no striking contrast in that respect; still there was for Constance a new magnificence in the sight of her father in his Indian quilted yellow silk dressing gown, with crimson facings and crimson silk cord and tassels. Then, too, he appeared in the very flower of health and prosperity. He had never looked so well as now, when his daughter, in answer to the voice of trouble he had sent to her, gave up every re-solve she had worked so hard to keep; and came, half broken-hearted with remorse, to his aid.

He looked up, all unaware of the pale face by the door, looked impatiently towards that door, and encountered suddenly his child's eyes. For an instant he was held mute and moveless by their gaze, so severe was it, so inexpressibly mournful, yet, withal, so loving.

What did she mean by that look? How dared she look like that? He grew a shade paler, and, trusting to work upon that love he saw flickering out like a light through the sternness of the face, he held out his arms.

"Constance, dear child, is it you?"

Two spirits were at war within her, and he saw it. He knew that one voice cried, "He has deceived me! He has acted a lie in order to get me here to dazzle and overpower me, and make me give 'Duke up." While another still more impetuously cried, "Let me go! It is my father holding his arms out to me, after all I have done against him—my father, whom I have not seen for years!"

Silent, and with a mask of love, he watched the conflict on her face, waiting to rule his actions according to the victory.

He had not long to wait.

"Father! father! father!"

She was down on the rug at his feet, sobbing out the name unuttered for years, clasping his knees with the vehemence of that little two-year-old child who used to cling to him with such wearying tenacity. He remembered even now how he could never take to the plain little thing, and how at times he had been half frightened of the heart beating under the baby pinafore with such strength of love, such passionate remorse for every little error it committed. He had often chid her harshly when she showed what he called an exaggerated sorrow for a fault. As she had grown older, it had at times seemed to Daniel Chorley that God had sent him this child in a spirit of chastisement, and to supply a certain faculty which he considered men with good sense and caution were as well, certainly more comfortable, without—namely, conscience. When he had been about to make some questionable business transaction, or to utter some commonplace white lie, just as other men asked themselves, "Can I do this on my conscience?" he, scarcely aware that he did so, asked himself, "Does she know it? What will she say?"

Conscience is not a thing to be much loved; it gives us too much cause for fear; it vexes, exasperates us with its "still small voice." And so it was with Daniel Chorley, as he looked upon his conscience, his little daughter lying there at his feet, sobbing forth, in the fond repetition of that word, "Father! father!" all the pent-up love and secret anguish of years. He looked upon her, and he feared her still, for he saw she was the same.

Presently, something—it might have been the sparkling of his diamond ring in the firelight—recalled that look, which had so annoyed him, to her face again, and she rose up quickly. Before she could speak he took her hand, and said excitedly—

"Constance, I have not called you back to poverty and hard work; I am rich. Your mother's sister has left me everything—left 'Duke, I mean; she has left 'Duke everything when he comes of age; but meantime the property is in my hands for the benefit of us all. Yes, it is ours at last. We ought to have had it long ago. Colonel Armstrong, to whom the estates originally belonged, never acknowledged me when I married his younger and favourite sister,—your mother, you know. But, having no children of his own, and being very proud, and anxious about the perpetuation of his name and family, he would have taken my first-born child to be his heir, had he been a son. But you came instead; and so the chance passed away, for he left all to his eldest sister, your aunt, Jane Armstrong. Well, now, she, too, is dead; and in dying has behaved very properly,—I may say, handsomely,—in giving everything to 'Duke, who will have to take the Armstrong name when he comes of age.

" So you shall be a lady, Constance; yes, you shall have everything that money can give you; and your brother—ah, my boy, my clever little 'Duke!—he shall be a great man. Who knows, Constance, perhaps he may be a baronet one of these days? How is he? Is he much grown? Is he stronger? Why didn't you bring him? What's the matter? Good God, Constance! he isn't ill? Speak, girl, speak?"

"No, father, no!" she said, drawing back; "'Duke is well, but——"

"But what?" cried Mr. Chorley, impatiently.

"Father, he cannot be what you say!"

"What do you mean, Constance?"

"I mean, father, 'Duke must not come home.

Mr. Chorley took a turn or two up the room before he could quiet himself sufficiently to speak. She guessed what his thoughts were as he did so, and the tears stole silently down her cheeks. Meeting him half-way across the room, she laid both her hands on his arm, and said—

"Oh, why did you bring this up again? why did you make me speak the words that it breaks my heart to say? You shouldn't have deceived me, father! You shouldn't have deceived me! I thought you had been very poor and ill, and I could not stay away from you when you asked me to come, as if it were to help you and nurse you. Father, you are rich and well; you do not want us; let us go on in our own way; I cannot make what you say of 'Duke, but I will try and make him a good man."

There was a look of incredulous pity as well as anger in his face as he said—

" And you mean to tell me that you would really prefer continuing this beggarly kind of life to living here with every luxury ? "

" I do, father."

" And why, pray ? "

It was a foolish question to have asked; he felt so the instant it quitted his lips. His colour rose, but he waited for her answer with his eyes fixed defiantly on her face. She returned his gaze with one of sorrowful surprise.

" *Why*, father ? "

" Yes, *why ?* " he cried, stamping his foot with a sudden burst of rage. " Constance, this is too absurd ! Because I gave you my confidence, my——"

He paused a second at seeing the peculiar hysterical smile that flitted over her face, which seemed to say, " *Gave* me, father ! Did you *give* me your confidence that night ? "

"Because," went on Mr. Chorley, "because, I repeat, you have my confidence, do you think you are no longer my child? Listen, Constance. I tell you plainly, there has been enough of this; I have fully made up my mind to put an end to it. First, I want 'Duke; I can now give him chances that I have longed to obtain for him ever since his birth. I want you, too. It is necessary you should be trained and made fit to preside over my household, and you ought to be proud to do so; it is not many fathers who would desire to keep a daughter at home after receiving such treatment at her hands as I have at yours. But more than that, Constance, you must remember that one in my position has the world to consider. As things were, it mattered little in what relations we stood to each other; now it is very different. Such an arrangement as you are mad enough to want would create no end of wonder and gossip, and prove most damaging to my prospects. Come now, Constance," he continued, softening his tone a little as he saw the face looking whiter and more rigid, "give over thinking and acting for yourself—it is wearing you out, my poor child; you are but a child, and it is unnatural for you to take so much upon you. Think of the life you may lead—think of the pleasure you will have in watching 'Duke's progress—think of the attention you will attract in the world some day with such a brother."

Poor Constance listened. She was wearied out with her long and toilsome night-walk, faint—for she had touched no food since noon—and dizzy with wonder at the good fortune which seemed to have fallen upon her father by magic. She was, therefore, at this moment, in no very heroic frame of mind. Fearful of erring either way, she listened until he had ceased speaking, and then sat some seconds in bewildered silence.

She sat so perfectly still, and so pallid-looking, that Mr. Chorley, to assure himself she had not fainted, laid his hand on her shoulder, and said gently—

" Constance ! "

She took the hand, laid her cold cheek upon it, and said, with a fresh burst of tears—

" Oh, father! dear father! you shouldn't talk to me of being rich; I haven't any care for it, indeed; *that* would never blind me or make me act wrongly; but when you talk of 'Duke, and of his new position, and what it might do for him, I don't know how to think or what to do. And when you say you want me, father, and think that I could do for you now in this grand place as I did there at home—when you say this I feel as if it would break my heart to keep away; but still, father, still I fear—I fear. It seemed so plain to me when I did this that I ought to do it —so terribly plain."

" Well, Constance, I am glad to hear you talk sensibly at last; now, perhaps, there may be some chance of bringing you to reason. As I have said before, you must remember that there was not the least occasion for me to make this appeal to you—in the eyes of the world, not the least— for I had every right to command you; but wishing to avoid the possibility of any recurrence to that painful subject in the future, and wishing, as I always do, to consider your feelings, I

thought it best to bring you here thus, and come
to a right understanding with you at once.   And
now listen to me."

And as well as her utter weariness, and her half-
happy, half-fearful agitation would let her, Constance did listen while he talked of his plans, and
gave her the particulars of the inheritance.   The
only thing of all he said that she clearly understood
was, that he intended to return anonymously, or
under the name of conscience-money, a certain
sum to a certain office; and, hearing that, she
laid her hands under her cloak, palm to palm, and
in one long sigh all her soul rose in prayer to
God for his blessing on the deed.

From that instant she felt her fate was sealed,
and she sat a little while, calm and still.   Mr.
Chorley went to a sideboard to get her a little
wine, and when he brought it he found her
gazing round wildly, with her hands pressed to
her forehead.   In that moment a sense of all
the change had come rushing upon her brain so
overwhelmingly, that she felt it failing her.

"Is it true?   Am I at home?   Is it all true?"

she murmured; and before Mr. Chorley could extend an arm to save her, the figure fell forward, and lay, in its shabby clothes, cold and still as death, on his rich carpet, and he stood looking at it, sorely bewildered, for he did not like to call the servants.

CHAPTER XIII.

CHRISTOPHER did not return to Peeler's Pond that night, but about two hours after he had seen Constance Chorley enter the terraced house at St. Clement's he went back to seek a lodging in Todness; but Kit did not sleep. He kept wide awake and restless the whole night long—so restless, indeed, that when the first peep of day showed him the mast-tops nodding in the fresh breeze behind the little black houses, his endurance was at an end; and, rising, he put on his clothes, removed the cockleshells and seaweed which decorated the window-sill, and, opening the window, let himself drop lightly on to the yielding shingle.

Kit turned his face in the direction from which the wind blew, because it was so strong and unfailing that he could almost lean his hot brow upon it, and that direction chanced to be St. Clement's.

Now there was, only a short distance from Mr. Chorley's house—which half a century ago stood alone on St. Clement's shore—a kind of rude beach chamber. A line of rocks, a groyne, the sea, and the huge sea-wall guarding the town promenade, were its four boundaries; and its yielding floor, strewn at each tide with fresh sea wonders, changed in light and colour with every change of the fitful sky that formed its roof. At early morning, when a faint tinge of rose-light came stealing along the cold grey sands, and the limpet-covered rocks threw their pointed shadows on the wet shingle, there was an air of elfish mystery about the spot, as though wild sea spirits had held their revelries there all night. In the glare of noon it was like a beautiful garden perishing for rain. The seaweed rustled as the breeze touched it, lifting it mockingly, as though to bear it to the sea, then dropping it again, and leaving it to dry and wither in the sun. The shell-fish shrivelled in the shell, the star-fish grew limp on the hot stones, and along the bleached road of the groyne came thousands of creeping things in search of prey, and the dead fish was black with sunflies.

But at night, when every separate pebble was made lustrous by the heavy sea dew and the moonlight, and the sands grew white in patches and circles, as if they were being dried by the feet of invisible dancers, then all the great sea seemed to turn to it in a passion of remorse for its neglect, prostrating itself before it with great cries, and adoring it with mysterious song—now sweet and tender, and accompanied with gifts fresh from its deep treasure-hold; now wild and complaining, and a savage snatching back of all, and then again stealing on doubtfully with low sobs and inarticulate murmurs, or only a' sound like the throbbing of a heart too full for utterance. All the withered and impure things it swept away; and in their place strewed fresh fair shells and seaweed, in feathery garlands of soft sea colours and rich bars of greenish gold, and so decorated it till it appeared a strip of a new and wonderful land.

Here, in the grey dawn of the Sunday morning, the only restless thing to be seen, save the sea and the dipping sea-gulls, paced Christopher Vallon.

It was a new place to him, but was such a spot as we all of us have somewhere—a corner of the wide earth wherein to come as to a temple, and let the soul unveil.

Something had passed out of Christopher's life during this night—something the presence of which he had never owned, but which had been with him for five years, and never, whether at his work, or in his walks, or in his dreams, never leaving him. It had stolen over his life imperceptibly, like faint February sunshine over a landscape, which deepens so gradually in intensity that we hardly know it is the sunshine, making it beautiful until the sun goes down, and leaves it cold and grey.

As the first sickening sense that he had endured such a loss came upon Christopher he was bewildered, and attributed it to the close atmosphere of his little room; but when he found that it followed him out into the fresh air, and pressed upon him closer and closer, he turned upon himself fiercely to know what it meant; he took it with him into this wild, wrestling chamber of his, which had seen him throw many a strong enemy —fierce pride, bitter disappointment, and sore despondency—but never a one like this. Nevertheless, he defied it scornfully, and grappled with it with all his strength.

But in vain, poor Kit; this was not to be thrown—this was not to be numbered amongst his triumphs.

Exhausted with walking up and down ankle-deep on the beach, he threw himself on the groyne, and buried his face in his hands. The tears came into his eyes—tears, not of pain, but of shame and vexation, such as he had shed often on these stones before, when forced to bow to the sway of passions he felt unmanly, and whose power he had denied until they overwhelmed him. Not that he bowed before this antagonist. No;

though it proved too strong for him now, he would never surrender; he would starve and mortify, weaken and crush it by degrees, but never surrender.

So, sitting down upon the groyne, he amused himself with looking scornfully at the loss which this enemy, this dragging pain at his heart, the like of which he had never felt before, would fain make him believe he had sustained.

It had come upon him, this pain, with the closing of the door of that grey house upon a slender figure in black; and had clung to him tenaciously through all these intervening hours, crying to him to behold how a sudden shadow had swept over his life; and how that success, which yesterday made him feel such quiet, happy strength in himself, now stirred in him nothing but scorn. And at this moment, when Christopher, in spirit, shook his fist at it, and defiantly bade it show him to the uttermost that loss of which it raved, it answered him with such a storm of mournful, passionate eloquence that he was stupefied, hardly able to credit that the voice proceeded from the depths of his own being, and sat listening as though it were the sea that spoke, or some other separate and distinct thing.

"What loss? what loss?" it said; "go back into life and work again, and by slow and painful degrees thou shalt discover. If, indeed, thou art ignorant now of the hope, dim and unconfessed, which thou hast cherished, which hath kept thee subdued and earnest at thy work, then all the more shall thou be haunted by its ghost, now that it is dead. It shall meet and greet thee at all times and at all places where it hath been with thee before, and whereat thou hast disowned it. It shall meet and greet thee, this dead hope, in the image of a sweet, pale face thou knowest, at busy street corners, in thy work-room, where it was with thee, though thou didst deny it, giving cunning to thy hand. Open the ledger, and it shall smile faintly upon thee through the figures; go where thou wilt, it shall be with thee, and thou shalt know it for a ghost, the reality of which is gone, for ever gone!" And the sea waves, breaking in mournful rhythm at his feet, repeated, "Gone, for ever gone!"

"Gone, for ever gone!" they said; and Kit, in listening for one moment, took his foot from his enemy's neck, for one moment only; but in that moment it leapt up, measured its strength against him, and he fell—fell, writhing under the shame, the half-terror of a man who feels a part of his being, hitherto held in subjection, all at once assert itself and overwhelm him utterly. To Kit—Kit, with his happy scorn for all sickly sentiment, all unhealthy affections, this was actual pain.

He crushed his face against the stones, genuine and vehement in his surrender as he had been in his resistance; nay, even finding in that surrender a wild throe of delight mixed with the shame; and he knew not which it was that made him tremble all over, as, muffling his voice in the stones, he cried—

"It is true I love her! I am a fool! I love her!"

Now once confessed, it was not in Kit's nature

to try to diminish his love in his own eyes ; on the contrary, since he had to bear such a burden, he would rather see in it a thing ennobling to him to bear than disgraceful and mean. So he rose and sat on the groyne again, and looked upon his love, measuring its strength as we measure the strength of an antagonist, with pride as well as awe, seeing that if we conquer at all the conquest shall be no mean one.

The sun was rising large and radiant between the sea and the jagged point of the last cliff, colouring all the grey, cold line of coast; and as Christopher sat shivering under the warm, soft glow that slowly penetrated through his wet clothes, he found that his love in like manner so tinged all his memory that he could in no wise discover the exact point at which it had begun. Not that he made any great effort at doing so. Since he dared not, for a moment, take his love into the future, it was sweet, dangerously sweet, to carry it back, and let it invest the past with a beauty that never really belonged to it—to live over again every incident that had brought them together, with the emotions he would have felt had his love then existed.

As for Constance herself, he tried in vain to remember the time—and there undoubtedly had been such a time—when he had thought her plain, awkward, and secretive. Ah, now the very defects in the face that floated before him only served to individualise its beauty, to round it, and keep it utterly distinct from all other faces, and cut it deeply into his memory. How perfectly he knew it—every line, every thick, rich wave of hair slanting from the forehead! He always saw the head a little bent, as if with that secret burden which she bore, and the forehead already bore signs of hard mental conflict; but for this the sweet half-smile of patience about the mouth and chin, and the depths within depths of happy faith in the dark eyes, made all amends; and the face, whatever it might have been some five years back, when Kit could not or would not remember it, was, in the bloom of its eighteen years, exceedingly sweet and comely to look upon, and that not through Christopher's eyes alone.

Perhaps it was this quality of faith in Constance which first drew his thoughts towards her; for Kit himself, as he encountered failure after failure, had gradually exchanged faith for obstinacy; and, though obstinacy had in this case brought him success, it was not the same kind of success as that achieved by faith. Obstinacy could send him to his work at regular hours, could keep him up over his books half the night, but it could not let him aspire—it kept all his ideas narrow and confined. And when he chanced to make before Constance some deprecatory remark, half jesting, half serious, about his future, she would turn her eyes upon him for a moment with that gaze so full of faith in him, that, meeting it, his spirit was at once humiliated, yet raised. With those eyes upon him, he felt a thirst to be yet true to the dreams of his childhood—almost a belief that, under their influence, he could be; and they were good dreams, for Kit's childhood had been worthy of the name—healthy, pure, and advancing as the footsteps of spring.

And thus, as I have said, gradually, almost

imperceptibly, something had flowed into Kit's life, strengthening and widening its whole current, and he never knew it—no, never until now, this Sunday morning, when he sat upon the beach, watching the sea wakening in its wintry magnificence, and felt it gone, for ever gone.

And then, with a keen joy pricking through his anguish, came the assurance that, until this barrier rose up between them, a large place in that loving hidden heart was his. The barrier itself, was it so great it could not be crossed? No; but, being on the side he was, his pride forbade his moving a thought towards it, so he withdrew his eyes from the great grey house to which he had lifted them, and bent his head in submission once more to the monotonous rhythm of those green, hollow waves that still repeated, in the sunshine as in the gloom, "Gone, for ever gone!"

A heart pure and faithful as the angels, strong and passionate as his own, "Gone, for ever gone!"

He heard footsteps on the beach behind him,

but he could not look up—no, scarcely to save his
life could Kit have looked up with that misery
upon his face; so, with his head still bent, he
began throwing stones at the waves, as if in one
of those fits of dreamy vacancy that will so often
come over us when close to the sea, and the
waves seemed to laugh mockingly as he threw at
them, still repeating, " Gone, for ever gone !"

Fiercer and fiercer grew Kit's conflict with the
waves.

But again there came upon his ear a sound as
of stones falling lightly together under the
pressure of a footstep—a footstep which a sudden
quickening of his pulse told him he should surely
know. The footsteps approached nearer, and the
nearer they came the more intent Kit grew in his
battle. What had she come for, if this were
really she ?—and he knew well it was no other—
what had brought her here in search of him
except some suspicion of his secret ? He
dropped the stone he was going to throw, expe-
riencing a sudden and violent revulsion of feeling
towards her. If that were so, he would soon

undeceive her—he would marry Madgie to-morrow but he would undeceive her.

He rose and turned round, but somehow, though he had a superstitious dread of her setting foot in this spot, lest the very stones should reveal what he had suffered here, he could not move to meet her—he could only stand and watch her coming swiftly along in the sunshine close by the glittering sea—watch her with a vague sense of its being the first time he had ever beheld her with his own eyes open to his love, and also with a sense that was not vague, but sharp and bitter enough, of its being the last time he should ever see her thus, in her poor simple dress, which he loved because it seemed a part of herself.

The last time! Oh, little Poplar, not so swift, not quite so swift, along the shining beach!

She was up to where he stood almost before he knew it, for he had been looking at her as at a thing afar off; and now, as he saw her smiling and stretching out her hand for him to help her down from the groyne, he took it as in a dream, forgetful of all his anger and vexation at her coming.

"Oh, Christopher, I'm so glad you've not gone home! Do you know about us? Have you heard all about it?" she said, springing down and sitting with him on the groyne, while looking at him with a mixture of childish curiosity and a half-misgiving as to what he would think of it if he did know. "Christopher, have you heard?"

"Oh, yes," answered Kit, attacking the waves again, to break that old, monotonous measure of their song, "Gone, for ever gone!"

"Christopher," she said, after they had both been silent a minute, during which Kit had searched in vain in his own heart for some cause of anger against her with which to arm himself, "there is a great deal I should like to talk to you about, but now I mustn't stay a minute scarcely. I was ill, faint, or something, last night, and it would make them anxious if they knew I had come out, so I want to get back before they know it. I was so pleased when I saw you from the window, I was obliged to come now, because I didn't know when I might see you again; and there is something I must tell you, Christopher: it is about your father and mother. First I must beg your pardon for helping to deceive you; and, mind, I should never have told what I am going to tell if it hadn't been for this change. Christopher, it's all nonsense about Tommy having taken to kicking, and about the boy your father used to have being sick. The truth is, he's been obliged to part with them both, and a great many other things besides, to live at all. Oh, they have been pinched and pinched! and I have had to see it, and yet be unable to help them—sometimes even a burden on them. But now I can help them; and, Christopher, the first bit of pleasure and pride I have had in being rich came over me as I remembered this. At first I am afraid I was dreadfully ungrateful. I've lain awake all night nearly, feeling as though I had fallen into a strange world where I could find no corner to rest in; but this morning, as it began to get light, I remembered them, then I felt glad.

While I was wondering whether you had gone home, I saw you from my window up there; and now, Christopher, if you please, I have come to ask your advice about how I am to begin."

To all this Christopher listened, feeling that weapon which he held against her—the thought that she suspected his love—grow looser and looser in his grasp with every word, and at last slip from it altogether. He ceased throwing stones, for fear she should see the trembling of his arm. He was touched—ay, touched to the very core—by her coming to him in this way, so simply—trustingly—so unlike all the world. Any one else would have been fearful of giving offence, and gone to it in a roundabout way: here, again, was her marvellous trust.

But though, while she was speaking, Christopher could not help a wild delight in that trust penetrating his whole being, yet when she had finished, and he must answer her—like the wolf at the fountain, who was determined to find cause of anger against the lamb, or immolate her with-

out cause—he began to view her words in quite
another light. So, while he had been away, his
father and mother had let her see them pinch
and starve that money might be sent to him!
He thanked them for that, certainly. And now
she came to tell him of it, and offer to undo the
mischief he had done—she, the houseless wan-
derer they had taken in—she, to play the patro-
ness over them! There was beginning to rise in
him a bitter antagonistic spirit he had never felt
before.

"Well, Christopher, tell me," she repeated,
"how am I to begin?"

"I scarcely understand you," he answered with
a slow coldness that seemed to freeze the blood in
her veins. "Were you offering to lend my father
and mother money—to give them an almshouse—
or what?"

She rose from the groyne where they were
sitting, and looked at him, half-terrified by his
cruel tone.

"Christopher!"

"Miss Chorley!"

She burst into tears, and, moving a step or two back, said passionately—

"Christopher, how can you, how dare you, speak to me like that? You know me better—you must know me better! What have I said? They took me in a stranger; we have suffered poverty and trouble together; and now, since to one good fortune has fallen, must not all share it? Don't they deserve it more, much more, than I?"

The wolf had almost reached its last resource, and would, perhaps, have to annihilate the lamb without a cause, after all. With a short, sarcastic laugh, which went through her as coldly and cruelly as sharp steel, Christopher answered—

"Your charitable notions are confused just now; but no doubt your father and your friends will soon set them right, and show you a wiser way of disposing of your money. As for us, when we are in prison for debt, or growing burdensome on the parish, we may, perhaps, come to you for a little assistance; but, until then, I think not."

"And this, then—this is really your answer, Christopher Vallon?"

Kit ought to be forgiven if he did take a kind of brutish pleasure in the dry, proud agony of her tone. He ought to be forgiven, for he himself, in his innermost heart, was suffering in prospect of the dreariness and desolation of the years to come. How he answered her he knew not; it seemed as if some black raven beside him croaked reply, instead of his own voice speaking.

"It is; your assistance is declined, with all thanks, of course."

"Very well; let it be so. Good-bye, Christopher."

Good-bye? He could not speak it; but she did not wait; he thanked God she did not wait. He heard her sharp, crisp step on the little stones, moving onwards, and he was thankful, for his hypocrisy was at an end; the raven at his side had spread its hideous wings and flown—had not even stopped to croak "Good-bye." He was alone. Had he suffered thus, had he thus lied in spirit, for the sake of his own pride, and that alone? Not so—not so, indeed. The deathlike peace of utter misery was upon him for an instant, and it said to him, with white lips and voiceless whisper—

"Be still; thou hast done well; for thine own sake and for hers thou hast done well. Had she guessed thy love it might have cost her dear. Come, then, take comfort in the thought; look thy last, and be at rest!"

And he clenched his hands in hard submission, and lifted up his face and looked.

The moisture in his eyes, and the sunshine together, made a golden mist between him and her, and looking through it fixedly he watched the slight, dark figure gliding, gliding away—his first love, his life's sole hope, there in the morning sunshine, gliding, gliding away!

The Present was too small to hold his misery, and it went shivering forth, disturbing all the Future, till through that golden mist which rose between them he seemed to see slowly stalking, one by one, phantoms of the years to come. And watching, it appeared to him that all those years

had really passed; that he was an old man looking back instead of forward—back upon that sun-
shiny morning of his youth, when the sea glittered,
and a thousand diamonds flashed out to the sun
along the orange beach, and the rose-light crept
along the grey sands—saw himself sitting there
on the groyne in the vigour of his youth, watching his love moving on, and on, away from him
farther and farther, yet sitting there still, dumb-
stricken, powerless; and it seemed to him, moreover, that he, in his old age, was, as he looked
upon the picture, moved to stretch forth his
arms towards that form fleeting through the
golden mist—to stretch forth his arms, and to
lift his voice with a great cry of remorse and
agony—

"Constance!"

Kit hid his face in his hands, and shuddered.
It was no voice of age that had escaped him, that
went vibrating along the beach, but her name
uttered with the full power of his lungs.

The crisp, light footfall ceased. He would
almost have cut off his right hand to have been

able to recall that mad cry, for the next instant his heart shook rather than beat.

They came nearer, those slow, timorous footsteps—they paused by him—there was a sound as of the slender figure dropping on its knees—a sense of a heart near him, shaken with as great a trouble as his own. But he could see nothing; his face was hidden in his hands.

The mystery of his grief was awful to her, and a prophetic thrill of the truth shot through her as she laid her hand on his wrist, and said—

" Christopher !   Kit, dear Kit !"

He looked up; her face was there, close to his, looking into it. It was enough. No word, no cry, only a stretching forth and meeting of hands, finger through finger, palm crushing palm; his brown eyes, splendid with the love and hope new-risen in them, looking up into hers; and hers with all the sea tints flashing in their dark depths, looking down into his. So they read the love of each other's heart.

That breaking of the waves, which a minute ago had fallen on his ear like a dirge, now seemed to have become the very pulse of their dumb bliss—bliss all the more intense because they dared not let it look forward—because it must all be condensed into those few, brief, full moments.

And the sun shone, and the sea glittered beneath it, and those moments ebbed away. Kit felt the last one in which they had to be together was come, and he let his face fall on the hem of her black dress, gripping her hands tighter and tighter.

As for Constance, she could feel no anguish even in parting; the joy that had risen in her heart seemed strong and enduring as the morning sun, and threw a golden pathway over the troubled waters of her life. Like this sun, truly, it might set—might be obscured by nights of stormy darkness, or by nights thick-set, as though with stars, with keen, bright-pointed spears of wholesome pain. All this might be, yet, assuredly, it would rise again and again, renewed in beauty and freshness every time, until it rose into that sky where it could never wane. So there was no sadness in her voice, only tremulous happiness, as she laid her hand on the rich chestnut hair, with something of a mother's pride in its beauty, and said—

"Come, Christopher, I must go."

He looked up, and, meeting her smile, sunnier and more exquisite than the gleam of primroses or daffodils, he could not forbear smiling also, or being stirred like her with a sense of the immortality of love.

They rose and stood holding each other's hands, and Kit felt his anguish and doubt coming on him again.

" Give me something, Constance—something to take home with me to look at, and remember it's all true."

" Certainly we must give each other something; but look, here is my pocket empty. I must buy you something as splendid as can be got for money, and send it to you."

"No, no; I will have none of that," said Kit, almost angrily; " I want something that belongs to you now, not bought with that money."

" Well, then, take this," she said, laughing, and

pulling off a little crape rosette from the body of her dress; "and remember, whenever you look at it, that I have sworn by the hand that made it— which was your mother's—to be true to you while a shred of it lasts. And now what have you for me? Something better than that, I hope."

"Nothing that you will care for as I shall for this little fool of a bow, but something, none the less, which has cost me an awful lot of money; and which, if I don't see round your neck every time I meet you in your carriage here, while I am sneaking past about my business, I shall request the loan of to strangle myself with. There it is. I meant to have given it to you with the other presents last night."

She held a glittering chain of gold in the sun.

"Not care for it, Christopher? Why, it is magnificent! Well, it may be hard for me to manage, perhaps, but I don't care; I promise you solemnly you shall never see me without it."

"That's enough. Good-bye!" said Kit, turning away, and throwing himself down on the beach.

"Good-bye," she said, stooping and giving him her hands. "Good-bye, my friend—my next to God!"

He pressed them to his eyes and lips, then threw them from him, saying hoarsely—

"Good-bye. Go, Constance, go!"

She turned away and ran up the beach, hiding the chain in her dress.

CHAPTER XIV

KIT'S STONY HILLS.

THE snow had been falling thinly, and the greyhound weather vane had set its tail persistently against the north, from which, all day, blew a fine profitable wind—a wind that wafted every stray passenger along the Iversham road, on horse or on foot, under the creaking signboard of " The Waggoner's Rest."

But though, owing to this fact, and the landlord's good temper in consequence, the kitchen looks more inviting than usual this evening, it is not here we must stay.   Let us look in with Mrs. Standish upon the fine old gentleman who paces up and down the dark little best parlour, waiting for 'Duke's return from school under the care of Kit as the Vallon representative.   Everybody in the house comes to peep at him, as the father of the two little outcasts found by Jemmy on that memorable April morning in the sackroom. His daughter has come with him, and sits in the dark window, thinking of many things.

It was about four of the cuckoo clock in the bar—just when the pacings up and down in the best parlour were heard to get restless—that Kit came quietly into the kitchen—quietly, but not alone. The old gentleman heard—pushed past Mrs. Standish in the passage—and received his boy, flushed and trembling, in his arms.

Humphrey Standish and his wife had argued great things for Kit, from the old gentleman's expressions of boundless gratitude to the Vallons for their kindness to the children. Madgie, too, as she sat trimming her Christmas cap, near the till, ready to take money from her father, and give change, closed her pretty eyes, more than once, over a picture that was very pleasant to look at; a group, in the best parlour, of herself and Kit; and that kind silvery-haired old gentleman, joining their hands, and settling upon them a handsome annuity for life.

Such dreams, however, did not seem to be at all in the way of realisation that night. No sooner did Daniel Chorley hold his boy safe and sound in his arms, than his feelings regarding Kit experienced a complete reaction. After all, he reasoned with himself, this young man had shown a very unnecessary officiousness about the whole matter, which looked rather like a wish to lay him, Mr. Chorley, under personal obligations to himself; and this, after certain suspicions Constance's way of mentioning Kit had awakened in him, was not to be endured for a moment. Therefore, though his gratitude had, in a great measure, vanished, when he sent for Kit into the parlour, he determined to reward him handsomely, and to have done with him, and all his daughter's low connections, at once and for ever.

When Kit, without appearing to be either surprised or insulted, quietly declined taking the three bank-notes held out to him, the old gentleman fixed upon his face a suspicious and offended glance.

" Yes, yes, young sir," he said, in a tone of

offended dignity that Humphrey Standish, who was listening at the door, thought very fine indeed, in reproof of his nephew's careless, independent sort of manner; "yes, yes, young sir, this is all very well; but allow me to remind you it is not right to me, this unbusiness-like behaviour."

"Not right to you?" asked Christopher, lifting his eyebrows with affected surprise.

"Because, by refusing what is due to you for this service you have rendered me, you necessitate my remaining under an obligation to you."

"Yes; that is true, certainly, but can't be helped, sir," said Kit, shaking his head. "But still, Mr. Chorley, if at any time I should know of a way in which you could help me, I promise I will give you a chance of removing your obligation (as you will call it so) by making you acquainted with it. Good evening, sir. Miss Chorley, good-bye."

"Well, certainly," remarked Mr. Chorley, as the door closed upon Kit, "that is the most presuming, absurd young man it has been my fate to meet. Come, 'Duke, my boy, let us be going."

" And would they part like this ? " Kit asked himself, when he was alone.

The moonlight streamed in clearly at both ends of the red brick passage; by the door of the garden, where he had pulled radishes with Madgie that April morning under the apple-trees, and by the front door with the square table box-tree on each side. It was against one of these that Kit leant; and before his feet, on the close, thick grass, lay the shadows of the low railings. On the road without all was very silent, so silent that he could hear the cows munching in the fields opposite, the same slanting fields he had walked up with *her* from the river side long, long ago.

But neither the silence nor the moonlight, pouring upon him through the gaunt bare chestnut boughs, like a smile of peace, stilled the bitter and contemptuous feelings that were beginning to surge and swell in Kit's breast. It seemed to him that had Constance's father been a sultan or prince, the distance between them would have been less than it was now, with this intense dislike which he found already rankling in him against Daniel Chorley, and which he had just seen was heartily returned. It had been a hard struggle to keep his voice even and unconcerned, and his words respectful, in that brief intercourse which had just passed; and to which he had gone expecting, at least, the outstretched hand of common gratitude.

Had such a hand been held out to him, Kit, in spite of a vague, instinctive aversion of many years' standing, would have taken it with right good-will; both because it *was* her father's, and because he had a real desire to grasp it, as the hand that might give or withhold his life's happiness. Not that Kit, however things might have turned, meant to accept that happiness without first earning it, by the attainment of a position in the world, that it would be an honour to ask her to share with him. And, between the day he could do that and now, there lay, oh, how

long a space of sickening doubt, and effort,—
sometimes to be rewarded, but more often vain;
of hope, and disappointment; of faith; and faith
such as his, with its strong, but fitful pulse, is
not altogether a thornless flower to wear at one's
heart; all this Kit had seen in the distance that
Sunday morning, as he journeyed along the beach
on the day of his betrothal. But as the great
light about him had made the sea and beach
appear boundless, and the houses of the town
small and far off, in like manner had the glow of
new first love in his soul left in dim indistinctness
all that lay beyond the present. Later, when
that love could no longer live on remembrances
only, but began to pine for hope, he had looked
forward, and seen all this more clearly. It was
hard; yet, how could he complain? how do
otherwise than accept it, unmurmuringly? As
for work; he thought upon his strength, and
smiled! As for waiting; how old were they?
Eighteen and twenty-three. What was waiting,
what were years, to them? What manner of
man could he be, that would cry out at Fate,

if he might look up, after a year's toiling for
the woman he loved, and find her but nineteen;
and then, were his task not finished, might toil
for yet another year, and another, and another,
and find her still waiting for him, in the glory
of her womanhood?

And well considering these things in his
heart, Kit had prepared joyfully, fearfully, to
climb the rough, stony hills, that lay between
him and his life's fair promise.

How he had sped, his look and attitude,
as he leant heavily against the box-tree in the
moonlight, this Christmas Eve, showed plainly
enough.

It was not only that he had found the stones
so cruelly sharp this day, in the waiting to see
her depart from him, for neither knew how long
and weary a time, without a word or look of
leave-taking—without that silent, strength-giving
farewell of friends who depart separately, on long
perilous journeys—that silent farewell, in which
the sting of parting is half crushed out in the
mute, trembling, breathless pressure of heart

against heart, lip against lip. O yes! these stones of Kit's were sharp; they bruised and hurt him sore; yet it was not their sharpness that drove him back. It was, rather, the thought that all his labour for years to come must, to attain his end, be ruled so as to please a man whom he despised from his innermost heart; a man of whom he knew no one good thing. It was this that hung about the stones like a loathsome slime, and made his feet slip and fail on them; and, once beginning to doubt and recoil, everything he had stood upon as being immovable seemed to totter and fail him. He doubted himself, he doubted her, doubted whether he had not acted selfishly and rashly, thus to burden her life with a tie that must bring her so much pain, and secret uneasiness, and weary waiting. Would her trust in him, and her love, outlive that waiting? A something—perhaps the spirit of that love and trust he doubted—made him answer, in a still, small voice, full of pained tenderness—

"It will, and thou knowest it—it will outlive all things, all time!" But Kit, in his blind and savage fit of doubt, giving his own heart the lie, cried, " I know better—it is impossible—I was a fool even to have thought of it—a fool and a selfish brute!"

Thus poor Kit, as he lay groaning in spirit at the base of those stony hills of his, wanted to persuade himself it was better to set his foot upon them no more, to give up all the fair promise that was beyond them, and use all his strength in forgetting it. If it be thought that, in all this, he was weak and wavering, let it be remembered of what his life had been up to the last five years —how painless—how unclouded—and how free; and now was it to be wondered at that he had great impatience and fear at this solitary, unfed, craving guest; this slow tearing away of self, and consecration of all thoughts and feelings to another?

" Was she too suffering?" he wondered. "Would she be glad of a word from him—as she passed from the door to the carriage—to free her?"

His anguish and restlessness, once settling into

that thought, made it press upon him harder and harder. It had come to him, at the sight of the carriage which Jemmy had just driven round. In another minute, Mr. Chorley, with 'Duke, wrapped up in furs, by his side, came out. The look with which he regarded Kit's lounging attitude against the box-tree was returned to him, with double contempt, by a pair of brown haughty eyes, the like of whose fierceness he had never seen in eyes before. Yes, poor Kit could look out all his contempt now, for his mind was made up, and he only waited for the appearance of a certain form in the doorway to say the word which should make all this strange sadness of his life but as a dream.

But she did not come; second after second passed, and yet she did not come.

Daniel Chorley was still engrossed in wrapping 'Duke up in the carriage. Very likely he had told her not to come, until he went for her; and how was Kit to speak then? He lifted himself up from the crackling box, and went in-doors.

You would have thought it a drunken man,

feeling his way in the moonlight along the narrow passage, his steps were so heavy and uneven, and he seemed to be battling with something in the air with his arms, some spirit that pushed him back tenderly, lovingly, but which he still fought and pressed on against.

He got to the parlour-door, and saw a figure sitting by a red dull fire. Feeling his way in the dark—between the table and chairs—he stood presently on the hearth-rug, griping the mantel-piece with his shaking hand, till the yellow tissue-paper round the looking-glass frame shivered audibly.

She watched him in silence and half-terror, for he seemed to have risen up before her like a ghost. She scarcely dared to speak, or let him speak, feeling that her father would be standing at the door in a second. Kit felt it, too, and dared not be silent—no, not for an instant, though this little picture of her which the dull red firelight gave him, as it hovered about her head and sweet, sweet, fearful face, scarcely less pure-looking than the white rose resting on the waves of her dark hair inside her bonnet—though this picture of her was the one which would be with him for evermore, he dared not pause to stamp itself on his heart distinctly, but must content himself with bearing it away, all imperfect and shadowy as it was—must speak and part at once.

He bent down, taking her hands and wringing them, and then let them drop without a word, still bending over her. She could not understand his manner; his strong, hard-set face, his eyes bloodshot, as if some great strain were behind them. He woke in her a wild fear that made her forget all about her father.

"Constance!" She did not know the voice as his; and a sudden horror went through her of his finishing the sentence; so when he had only said "Constance!" she stood up, and pushed him off with both her hands, crying, in a low, beseeching voice — "Christopher! O my love, my love! what is it?"

And it came to pass that he did *not* speak the words he had come on purpose to utter. He drew her to him, and folded her to his heart, and took her into it and into his soul as he had never done before, to be one love through all existence, to be his wife "for better for worse, for richer for poorer." And thereto with tears, and low, passionate vows to God, did he plight her his troth.

Steps came, they parted hurriedly, groping their way on either side the table—Constance to meet her father at the door, Kit to find a little grimy horsehair sofa in the corner, and to fling himself upon it face downwards.

END OF VOL. I.

BRADBURY AND EVANS, PRINTERS, WHITEFRIARS.